T0098744

Victorious Heart

Endorsement

"Kim is my friend. A woman full of strength and grace. In spite of a heart-crushing tragedy, Kim has braved her way toward the Light. She didn't sprint past her pain, but Kim has waded into the pool of her reality and has come forth offering us hope."

Patsy Clairmont
Author of *You Are More Than You Know*

Victorious Heart

Finding Hope and Healing
After a Devastating Loss

KIM PEACOCK

NEW YORK

LONDON • NASHVILLE • MELBOURNE • VANCOUVER

Victorious Heart

Finding Hope and Healing After a Devastating Loss

© 2019 Kim Peacock

All rights reserved. No portion of this book may be reproduced, stored in a retrieval system, or transmitted in any form or by any means—electronic, mechanical, photocopy, recording, scanning, or other—except for brief quotations in critical reviews or articles, without the prior written permission of the publisher.

Published in New York, New York, by Morgan James Publishing. Morgan James is a trademark of Morgan James, LLC. www.MorganJamesPublishing.com

ISBN 9781642791891 paperback
ISBN 9781642791907 eBook
Library of Congress Control Number: 2018907983

Cover Design by:
Megan Dillon
megan@creativeninjadesigns.com

Interior Design by:
Christopher Kirk
www.GFSstudio.com

All scripture quotations, unless otherwise noted, are taken from the New International Version (NIV). Copyright 1984 by Zondervan.

Edited by: Christy M. Nunez
Photo taken by: Jonathan Olivares

Morgan James is a proud partner of Habitat for Humanity Peninsula and Greater Williamsburg. Partners in building since 2006.

Get involved today! Visit
MorganJamesPublishing.com/giving-back

Donna "Nicole" Peacock

Table of Contents

Foreword

"A person's days are determined; you have decreed the number of his months and have set limits he cannot exceed"
(Job 14:5).

Elevating hope for a family who has been stunned by a tragedy is what pastors do; or at least, try to do. As I walked into the church auditorium, now almost twenty years ago, I could feel the emptiness. The tragedy that brought us together that day involved a beautiful, God-honoring, seventeen-year-old girl. The grief was thick and the crowd was quiet. Her death seemed senseless to us all. No rhyme. No reason.

At the time I was the father to three teenagers myself. So, as I began, I was hoping my words to her family would even convince me there could be something good in it all. I began by saying, "Today we celebrate the life and death of two individuals, Nicole and Jesus." After all, if anyone could relate to the grief her family was feeling, it was God. His child was killed in a tragic circumstance, too.

As the service concluded, we were all thankful God's power had been evident, bringing joy with the sorrow, and declaring Nicole's clear testimony of faith in Jesus to the hundreds of people who were listening intently. But it had only been nine days since she passed.

When Kim asked me to write the foreword for *Victorious Heart*, the first thing I did was look for the notes I used at Nicole's service. I script every public message I give, yet I was still pleasantly surprised that, after all these years, I was able to find it. But even after reading again what I shared that day, both from scripture and my heart, I was still hard-pressed to remember much about those initial weeks. After reading Kim's manuscript for this book, those memories came flooding back in high-definition. What's truly amazing is that now, twenty years later, I wasn't reading about a tragedy, or even a family's hope in the wake of tragedy. I was reading about a stunning and complete victory over tragedy.

I'm not sure where it comes from, but so many of us have the impression we are somehow owed a certain number of years to live; that it's possible for someone to "die before their time." Perhaps we deserve eighty years. Certainly, at the very least, seventy...right? The truth is, none of us are owed anything. We get what we get. Actually, the Bible is pretty clear. All of our days are numbered before the clock even starts. Nicole Peacock's number was 6,430. When she and her family awoke the morning of December 28, 1998, none of them knew it. But Nicole's number was up.

Dr. Craig Barnes so eloquently wrote, "We will probably spend most of our lives with family, friends, good health and good work. But they are not ours by rights. They are not promised to us. We may have to give them back to God at any moment. Someday we will give them back. The trick is to learn how to do that before they leave us. That allows us to spend the rest of our time enjoying them as the temporary gifts that they are."

We talk about "defining moments" as if our lives are filled with them. No doubt, we experience many important events, even life-changing ones. But we call very few moments "defining" for a reason. They actually do define us. They create lenses through which anything and everything else we ever do is evaluated.

We could all write a book about surviving hard times. Invariably, we're all asked to. Everyone's story eventually includes at least a few difficult chapters. Sometimes those chapters show up near the beginning. Sometimes they surface later in life. But the choices we make in the confusion of those pages end up framing the way future generations remember us.

For the last twenty years, I doubt anyone in the High Desert Church family has thought of the Peacock family without processing those more immediate thoughts through the lens of this story. They became heroes to us. Tell that to them and they'll probably laugh out loud. Tell that to anyone else around here and they'll agree. After you read *Victorious Heart*, you will understand why.

I don't know why you chose to read this book. Maybe you love the Peacock family. Maybe you're writing a difficult chapter in your own story, or you're wondering what to say to someone who is. Regardless of the reason, prepare to be amazed. It's really not a story about a family who lost a child, but about the God who showed them how.

Tom Mercer

Senior Pastor, High Desert Church

Author of *8-15 – The World Is Smaller Than You Think*

Acknowledgements

I want to thank God for doing the impossible in my life. He has made me brave when I was a coward. He has given me words when I had none. He gave me hope when I was close to despair. He has made beautiful things out of my broken heart.

To my husband Larry who has walked this grief journey with me. You are my best friend and my biggest defender. Thank you for working so hard every day, so I can do what I do. You are amazing.

My daughter Megan. You have opened a tender, fragile part of yourself to help me with this book. Thank you from the depths of my heart. Nicole would be so proud of you. My son-in-law Jonathan. You inspire me to keep pushing through. Thank you for taking hundreds of photos of me for my headshot, because you wanted to get just the right one. You are a gift, not only to Megan, but to the whole family.

Ilene Walton, Kat Kirchner and my sister Donna Fedorka, thank you for proofreading the many drafts of this book and giving me honest feedback and encouragement.

A special thanks to those brave souls who in the midst of their own grief, quietly walked beside me during my darkest hours. There were many times I was so buried in my grief that I couldn't acknowledge their sacrifice, yet they still showed up. The gift of their presence sustained me and gave me courage to never give up.

To my amazing mentor and friend, Patsy Clairmont, thank you for encouraging me to go to the broken places to tell my story and for always reminding me I am more than I know.

I am so grateful for you Christy Nunez, and the gentle way you have edited this book. You knew what I wanted to say but didn't know how. Thank you for making a safe place for my heart.

Introduction

Words can't bleed.
They can't rupture.
They can't repeatedly drown in agony.

So, it will be hard for me to convey the depth of sorrow a parent wades in when their child dies. I can try. You can imagine. Yet whatever I say, and whatever you think, it's more...so much more.

Days after our daughter Nicole went to Heaven, we received a book mark from a dear friend. The top bore Nicole's name and underneath was the meaning of her name. Victorious Heart. Those were perfect words to describe our girl. I knew in that instant I wanted those words to be my mantra and theme for the rest of my life.

This book may be my unconscious attempt to eulogize my daughter. It may be yet one more attempt to assuage my guilt that I could not rescue her, or worse yet, that there was something I did or did not do as a parent that contributed to that fateful moment

My prayer for these pages is that if you have buried part of your heart in the soil of loss, you will feel heard. And in feeling heard be comforted. Look for **Grief Notes** as a special word from my heart to yours. Also, if you are the precious soul walking with a friend in grief, that you will be encouraged and guided. Take note of **Love Them Well**, advice from someone who has walked it on both sides, how to love your friends well.

Here, take my hand. You are not alone, we are not alone. We will survive...with a decided limp no doubt...yet in our time and way.

Hope is not fragile; just hard to find when the lights go out.

Chapter 1:

Simple Times

"Consider the lilies of the field..."
(Luke 12:27a).

P rior to December 28, 1998, we were a normal family with a normal life. Some of it messy, but overall, pretty typical for the average American, blended family. My husband Larry and I are the same age and went to the same high school, but we were just two kids among many, in the same place at the same time. After graduation and unknown to each other, we both married at a young age, each had a daughter and were divorced after two years. As Providence would have it, Larry was invited to the church I had attended from youth by his sister's friend. We soon noticed each other and realized all that we had in common including both being single parents of a young daughter. Mine, Nicole was three-years-old and Lisa, his, was two.

Larry later said he first noticed Nicole and me because Nicole was always so cutely dressed each Sunday for church. I, in turn, noticed Larry because he came in every week with Lisa sleeping in his arms. We soon started dating and married within a year.

Once Nicole and Lisa became sisters, they were instantly inseparable best friends. Their names were no longer spoken individually, as "Nicole" or "Lisa," but always spoken together as "Nicole and Lisa." Nicole took her role as a big sister very seriously and made it her responsibility to "take care of" her new little sister. Lisa was only a year younger (almost to the day) so they were often mistaken for twins. Contributing to this notion was the girls' sizes. Nicole, a petite brunette with blue eyes and freckles. Lisa has green eyes and inherited her father's blonde hair and tall, slender build.

Our first home as a newly formed family was a rented, one room house situated on ten acres in the high desert of Southern California. We had no heat or air conditioning, but we were young and it was all a great adventure. We didn't mind at first. Being a one room house and very limited on space, the landlord graciously gave us permission to close in the back porch and make it in to a room for the girls. Larry built each girl a hanging bed, so they had plenty of room underneath for playing and pretending. They spent hours in their room giggling and creating their own little world.

The girls were unaware we had no money and struggled to pay bills. Our church had a food bank that gave away free blocks of processed cheese. We consumed quite a bit of that free cheese. Many times, we were low on food when my mom would show up at the door with bags of groceries. She said she accidentally bought too much food at the grocery store. I remember thinking,

"Yeah right, Mom. How do you 'accidentally' buy too much food?". But we were grateful for those groceries and free cheese.

We loved making that little house our home during those first couple of years together. We learned to cope with the cold in the winter by hanging out near the bathroom with a space heater running or having the girls run laps around the couch before school. The fireplace also helped when we stayed near it in the evening before bed. It was a simple, sweet, poor time and I cherish every moment of those memories! In the midst of it, we were truthfully stumbling along as best we could, with little conscious faith in trusting God to provide. Yet in retrospect, we are amazed and humbled by God's repeated provisions.

There were times the adventure turned into alarm, like when I realized there was a bat hanging on one of the baskets on the ceiling of my kitchen. Needless to say, I freaked out and ran outside until Larry took care of it for me. I have had an aversion to bats ever since. There was also the time I almost stepped on a giant lizard running through the area we called our living room. I tore the house apart trying to get that thing out of there.

Larry, an earth-moving contractor, worked close to home in those days, so when I would have a crazy critter emergency, he could usually rescue me when he got home in the evenings.

Our business was small and sometimes he needed an extra person, so I would go help him by hauling equipment or running errands. One day he needed me to help him haul the backhoe, requiring me to drive a big dump truck pulling a trailer with a 16,000 lb backhoe on it. While I was focused on not running over anyone on the road, I was suddenly struck with a terrible pain in my lower abdomen and had to pull over. I told him I needed to go to the emergency room because of the extreme pain. He knew it was serious, because I didn't often consent to going to the doctor.

The hospital did some initial testing and found I had an ectopic pregnancy. (The egg is fertilized in the fallopian tube instead of dropping down to the uterus.) At that time, I didn't understand what that was. All I heard was "pregnancy" and was thrilled to think about having another child. Within moments, I went from joy to sadness as the doctor explained the baby would not survive and unless they did surgery, my life would be in danger as well. So, I had emergency surgery and tried to reconcile the fact that I would never have the chance to hold my baby.

I grieved that loss, even though I was only aware I had been carrying my unborn child for a few minutes. That experience gave me a heart for those mamas who have had miscarriages or those who carry their children full term, only to have their dreams dashed by the sometimes sudden and unexpected loss of those little ones. Deep sorrow comes with the loss of a child, at any age. Heartbreak can't be measured or should never be compared.

Through the pampering of my family, I got back on my feet and returned to the routine of life. About a year later, I began to notice the symptoms of pregnancy. I ignored it at first because I didn't want to get my hopes up. I didn't tell anyone, but decided I needed to do a home pregnancy test. I was both delighted and fearful when the little plus sign appeared on the testing stick. After sharing the news with Larry, we decided I should go to the doctor to be checked out. The doctor confirmed the pregnancy and assured us our baby was growing in the correct spot. Coincidentally, or should I say divinely, my new doctor was the same one who took care of me during my ectopic pregnancy and celebrated with us. We happily gave the girls and the rest of the family our wonderful news.

We realized during my pregnancy the little adventure house we lived in was no longer a good fit for our growing family and decided to move somewhere a little less adventurous. We bought two and a half acres and put a mobile home on it. I was so thrilled to have closets and carpet before our new little one arrived.

On February 13, 1987, our daughter Megan was born. We jokingly said we had "his, hers, and ours". Nicole, then five, and Lisa, four, loved their little sister and spoiled her rotten. Time flew and they were growing up before our very eyes. (I long for the sights and sounds of those days and the craziness of our busy household, even now.) I was trying to keep the kids focused on school while keeping up with our family's schedule. There were animals to feed, horses to ride and dance classes to take. In addition, the kids were involved in Awana along with other church activities and 4-H. "Happy Chaos," as Lisa used to call it.

Our kids had a blend of homeschooling and taking classes at our local charter school. Our earth-moving business had changed and expanded. Instead of focusing on a volatile residential and commercial market, we began to specialize in cemetery expansion and improvement. Larry had to travel more for work and our unique school situation gave us the opportunity to travel with him.

We had a full and content life as a family of five for many years when I heard a message about the overcrowding in Russian orphanages and the need for American families to fill in the gap through adoption. My heart was stirred and I wondered if the Lord was calling us to adopt a child from Russia. Larry wasn't so sure about the idea and told me he would pray about it. He did pray about it and the Lord pursued him on it for about three years. Every time he turned around, he was hearing about Russian adoptions. He finally asked the Lord for one more confirmation when he turned on the radio. Guess what they were talking about? Yes, Russian adoption. So, we began the year-long process and realized that about the time the Lord put adopting from Russia on my mind was about the time our new little son, Alexander was born.

We knew it was not a coincidence and were convinced in our hearts Alex was our son from the moment he was born. The ten-day trip in December of 1997 to Russia to pick him up was a bold endeavor that tested me in many ways. With the exception of Mexico, I had not traveled outside of the United States, much less with a four-year-old that spoke no English. Yet this stocky, hazel-eyed blonde boy held all of our hearts before we even met him.

We were then a family of six (the kids were ages 16, 15, 10 and 4) and settled into our new routine. Instead of "his, hers, & ours," we became "his, hers, ours & theirs." Nicole started her senior year in high school and was a huge help with driving everyone to their classes and picking up food for us when I was too overwhelmed to cook. She and I were really close. I think that is because at the time, she was more like me than anyone else in the world.

She was very balanced for someone so young. She was compliant, yet strong. She and Lisa were still buddies and partners in crime. She spoiled Megan and Alex and made sure no one messed with them. I'm not saying she was perfect, but she was a remarkable teenager. She definitely had a mischievous streak and was usually instigating some form of "Supervised naughtiness," as my friend Terri called it.

Nicole loved to TP (string Toilet Paper in the front yard) the homes of her friends in the darkness of night. I wouldn't let her drive that late, so I would drive and help them TP their friend's homes. Now, don't judge me, it was all in fun and I knew our house would get TP'ed during pay back and we all agreed, they'd have to do the clean-up. We'd load up whoever was at our house and the four kids, armed with lots of toilet paper and sneak off to decorate their friend's houses. We often got caught and ended up running down the street giggling. A few nights later, we would hear noises outside our house and would run out to discover that we'd been hit.

Nicole and Lisa fancied themselves as the TP Queens and even decided to use their influence to get the younger kids involved in their escapades at horse camp. They decided it was a good idea to TP the tents of the other campers and got caught. The leader in charge wasn't as understanding as I was about the concept of TPing and Nicole's "Supervised Naughtiness" got all of them in trouble. Even after that, Nicole would have a line of younger kids following her at the horse shows like the Pied Piper.

Lisa, Megan and Alex would love it when Nicole drove them anywhere, because she would always pull her purple truck into the gas station and load up with Slurpies and snacks. They were fiercely loyal to one another. Don't get me wrong, they would fight like crazy, but when mom pulled up, they would all act like nothing ever happened.

I know I remember the good more than the craziness, and there was plenty of craziness. There were times I was frazzled and perpetually disorganized. Everything felt messy, sticky and noisy. But now, looking back I see it was a pure, simplistic time. I miss it. I wish I could go back and capture those times and savor them. I think so much of our lives are lost in the striving and caught up in the busyness of life.

It was during one of those busy seasons, a year after we adopted Alex and about three weeks before Christmas when Larry said the strangest thing to me. I was sweeping the kitchen floor and he said out of the blue, "We need to be prepared in case anything was to happen to one of our kids." Those words struck terror in my heart as I quickly pushed even the consideration of such a thought far from my mind. Just like most moms, my kids were my world and I believed deeply I was too weak to cope with anything like that ever happening to me. I dismissed it, thinking only "strong" people lost children. I told him God would not allow that to ever happen, because He would not give us more than we can handle and I could not handle that. I see now God was preparing us when those sentiments were placed in Larry's mind. I think God does that for us many times in our lives, but we rarely catch it.

I had no idea what I would be facing a few weeks after that. After Christmas, with decorations and wrapping paper strewn all over the floor and leftovers still in the fridge, we began to prepare for our family camping trip to Pismo Beach, CA. It was something we all were looking forward to, but I felt an unexplained anxiousness in my spirit. I chalked it up to fatigue from the holidays and the anxiety of trying to take care of household and family details before we were to leave. Lisa stayed behind because she was on the varsity basketball team at school and they were participating in a holiday tournament. She stayed at my parents' house next door and took care of the animals while we were gone.

It was December 27, 1998. I didn't realize it would be the last normal day for our family as we loaded up the truck and got on the road. I wonder how many moments we miss in our everyday life because we are consumed with the details of getting where we are going, instead of being present in our current situation? The truck was filled with delightful chatter and I could feel the anxiety of the past few days melt away as we drove north on the highway toward Pismo Beach. We happily ate snacks and talked about plans for the upcoming year. There were many activities we looked forward to in hopeful expectation.

Nicole had gotten a new show horse, Neon, and excitedly talked about all the horse shows she was hoping to attend. She loved all things horsey and had been working hard to qualify for the American Quarter Horse Youth World show. Megan entertained us with her comical antics, while Alex just took it all in.

We finally made it to our destination and met up with some of Larry's family, with whom we would be camping. After dinner with the family, we stayed in a hotel so we could get a good night's sleep before we would be sleeping in sleeping bags and tents for the next few days. I often hold on to the sweetness of that night as I recall the little things. We had two rooms at the hotel with an adjoining door between us. In my mind I can still recall the silliness taking place as I tried to get everyone calmed down and in their assigned sleeping spots. The kids kept going back and forth between the rooms goofing off. Exhaustion from the busy last few days and the long drive started to set in as we eagerly climbed in bed. My unsuspecting mind could not conceive what the next day would hold as I drifted off to sleep.

- *Grief Note.* Cherish the memories. Don't be afraid to recall the sweet times.
- *Love Them Well.* It's okay to talk about how life was before a tragedy.

Chapter 2:

The Accident

"We are hard pressed on every side, but not crushed;
perplexed, but not in despair"
(2 Corinthians 4:8).

D ecember 28, 1998, we woke up rejuvenated and ready to go camping. The weather at the beach was clear and glorious as we all climbed in our vehicles to head out to the sand dunes. With the sparkling ocean on our right and the sand dunes on our left, we drove along the beach that led to the rolling Oceano Sand Dunes. After finding the perfect camping spot, everyone pitched in to set up our camp in a circle with the fire pit in the middle. Nicole and Larry had some dad and daughter talks about relationships while they worked on an area for us to ride the ATV's by our camp spot. We relaxed at the campsite for a while and ate our lunch before venturing out into the dunes to play. We took turns on the rented quads, motorcycle,

ATVs and riding in the truck. Nicole was hanging back, letting everyone else take turns riding, when I encouraged her to get in there and make sure she took a turn. We found an ideal area to watch everyone ride around what we called a sand dune bowl on a high hill and parked the truck.

Before the kids took off on the ATVs, Larry made sure they all understood the dunes dropped off dramatically when riding directly away from the beach. It is difficult to see the size of a drop-off, so they needed to be extra careful when riding away from the ocean. Larry was riding his motorcycle, Nicole was on our three-wheeler and everyone else was taking turns on the four-wheelers. I was relaxed, enjoying the sun watching everyone ride around when I noticed out of the corner of my eye a three-wheeler riding away from the beach at a high rate of speed and was headed straight toward a large drop off into the bowl of the sand dune. I realized that it was Nicole the moment she went sailing off the sand dune and lunged head first down the forty foot drop off. We all watched in horror as she landed on her head with the ATV on top of her at the bottom of the dune. Everything was a blur as we rushed down to where she was. I can remember screaming as I ran toward her, "It's Nicole!".

Larry got to her first and pulled off her helmet. In that moment, my memories are captured in clear, vivid snap shots. The space between those snap shots are fuzzy and vague. The first snap shot is burned into my mind and it is of Larry turning around with Nicole in his arms. She was unconscious. My father-in-law jumped into action and drove our truck down to the bottom of the dune. I helplessly watched as they loaded her in the back of the truck and Larry jumped in beside her. I remember waving them on yelling "go, go, go". I stayed behind with Alex and some of the family.

I don't know why I didn't run and jump in the truck with them. Maybe I was afraid of what I would be facing or maybe I just didn't want to slow them down. I know I just didn't go. It was a split-second decision I've questioned, and sometimes regretted, since then...wishing I had been with my girl.

However, I do think the Lord was protecting me from having certain images burned into my mind. We called 9-1-1 as they headed toward the beach to meet the paramedics. Larry was in the back of the truck doing CPR on Nicole, while his dad drove, Megan was in the back seat of the truck with his mom. Nicole's boyfriend Kevin rode one of the quads behind the truck.

Some people in a jeep, who had witnessed the whole thing, came and offered to take me to the beach to catch up with our truck, while Alex stayed with my sister-in-law. As I rode in the back of a jeep with people I didn't know, I prayed out loud over and over. "Lord, please make her breathe, please make her breathe". The people driving were very sweet and told me that she was going to be all right. I knew in my spirit it was not going to be all right and tried to explain that to them. My words came out in a panicked, jumbled mess. We arrived at the beach and I saw the paramedics and crowd around our truck. I was terrified. I saw them working on Nicole and I desperately wanted to touch her. But I couldn't get to her. I could only get to her foot toward the end of the tail gate. As I touched her shoe, I begged God to let me keep her here with me. I saw Kevin sitting on the quad, head in his hands and went to him. He was beside himself with what he was witnessing. It was then I saw the expression on Larry's face. I realized how dire the situation was. But I also knew how powerful God was and that He could do anything. Miracles were His specialty.

The paramedics loaded Nicole up into the ambulance and Larry rode in the back with her. A ranger offered to drive me to the hospital. The entire drive to the hospital I was praying out loud, "Lord, please make her breathe" and the ranger reached over and touched my hand and said, "Don't quit praying". I am so thankful for that ranger. At the time, I deeply believed it to be a sign Nicole would be healed. Reflecting, though, I recognize how many times I remembered his words in the days that followed. Those words reminded me to never quit praying, because I would need God's continual strength in what I was about to face.

I do sometimes wonder if that ranger was not a ranger at all, but an angel. I tried to contact him after we got home, but no one could ever find a record of the ranger that drove me to the hospital.

When we arrived, we saw Nicole being wheeled across the parking lot and in the entrance of the emergency room. They took her back where doctors and nurses began to work on her. Larry and I were outside her room praying, when he prayed for God's will in this situation.

"No! We need to pray for her healing!" I protested. My heart wasn't willing to accept what my mind was telling me. They took us into a waiting room where we met up with some of the rest of the family. Megan started going into shock in the waiting room. That's when it hit me...she witnessed everything that had happened in the back of the truck. She saw Nicole's condition and her dad trying to save her sister's life. The nurses brought Megan a blanket to warm her up and stabilize her.

Shortly after, the doctor came in with a chaplain. The doctor gathered us around him and said very matter-of-factly, "Basically, she died at the beach". That was it. Nicole's death pronounced in a cold, flat statement. The chaplain asked if he could say "the

Lord's prayer" with us. I felt myself sinking into a dark place, out of which I could never climb. I told him no, that we wanted to pray to God from our hearts.

I believe that moment was a fork in the road for us, a place to make a critical choice. Maybe the ranger's words were still in my mind, "Don't quit praying". Whatever it was that the Lord used to prompt us to pray saved us that day. Our family circled together, desperately holding onto one another, with a full waiting room watching and began to pray in earnest for God to carry us through and keep us from despair. We could feel His presence descend on us and cover the crushing pain in our hearts with His mighty power.

After we finished praying, the nurses and hospital staff took our family to a special room. The room was a small, dimly lit space with a stained-glass window called a Family Room. Before December 28, 1998, I never considered that hospitals even had these types of places. A place out of the way and quiet where a family could try to begin to process the loss or impending loss of a loved one. The nurses came in and asked us if we wanted to see Nicole. I know for some people this gives them a sense of closure. But for me personally, I chose not to see her in that condition.

Maybe it was like me not riding in the truck or the ambulance with her, maybe I was afraid to face the brutal reality that she was gone. I don't know for sure, but I said at the time that I wanted to remember her fully living. Nicole was the kind of girl that lived, I mean really lived. She worked hard, laughed often and loved fiercely. That is who I chose to remember at that moment.

I have wondered many times if the choice not to see her was the right one. I have asked myself if the decision not to go in hindered my sense of closure. I don't think it did. I still struggle with memories of her accident and what took place shortly after. For me, I am thankful I don't have to add the memory of seeing her on the hospital table void of life.

However, I do believe there is no right or wrong decision as to whether we should see our loved ones after they pass away. I know an amazing, beautiful woman who told me she went to see her daughter who had been killed in a tragic car accident. She said that she hugged and kissed her daughter, and that she thought it was the only way she would have believed her daughter was gone. She felt it truly did give her the beginning of a sense of closure. The thing about grief, it is just such a personal road. There are no two situations or personalities exactly alike, so we all handle grief in our own individual ways.

After we told the nurse we didn't want to see Nicole, we did ask her to bring us a lock of her hair and her jewelry. She placed those precious items in an envelope and brought them to us. I didn't have the courage to open it for quite some time.

We then had to gather ourselves and prepare for the trip home. In the quiet seclusion of the hospital family room we were faced with the awful decision of how to break the news to Lisa, who was staying at my parents' house, next door to our home. We decided to drive home and tell her face-to-face.

I don't remember exactly when, but at some point, Larry's sister Cindy and her husband arrived with Alex and Nicole's dog Nala. It was the first of many times that we had to break the horrible news that Nicole had died. How in the world were we supposed to say those words? The hospital staff was so gracious to us and pretended not to notice that they were bringing a dog in. It was as if they wanted to allow us every possible piece of comfort that we could have, so they said nothing about Nala. She had been Nicole's constant companion since she was a puppy and looked around as if she were looking for Nicole before curling up under my chair.

Before we left the hospital, Larry took Alex to the bathroom. In the bathroom Alex turned to Larry and said "Papa, where's Nicole?" Larry told him that Nicole was in Heaven, to which Alex replied, "Is she happy?" Larry said, "Yes, very happy". Alex was content with that answer. A man came out of one of the stalls, hearing what had been said. Larry said he was choked up and crying as he went passed them. This reminds me that people are watching us as Christians and how we respond to life's situations.

I also think often of Alex's response to Nicole being in Heaven. I want to have that kind of child-like faith, to remember the truth of our lives here. The unmistakable truth that what we see here is not all there is. Since then, I don't like to say Nicole died, I usually say "She went to Heaven". It helps me to keep the right perspective and to remember she did not cease to exist on December 28, 1998. She just moved from Earth to Heaven. A simple, premature, change of address

As we walked out of the hospital, I was overwhelmed with two thoughts. First, it was astonishing to me that everything outside the hospital looked so normal, so unchanged, while everything had drastically changed within our lives. Shouldn't the world have stopped? Or at least gotten a little darker? The second thought was a question...how in the world was I going to leave my girl behind at the hospital? I tried to remind myself "she" wasn't there, that her soul was with the Lord. However, that little body had been with me for seventeen years. She was formed within my own body and had been by my side ever since. She was more like me than anyone in the world. How could I possibly leave her there? It did not feel right and I couldn't get over the feeling I was abandoning her. As our family walked out to our truck, I had difficulty putting one foot in front of the other. I literally had to will my feet to move away from the hospital and to the truck. Once inside, we began that excruciating long drive home.

I had asked Larry's mom Arlene to ride along with us. She was an amazing prayer warrior, with a calm, peaceful spirit. She was a tremendous help on that tedious drive. She didn't say a lot, but I knew that she was fervently praying for us. She lovingly helped with Alex and Megan, offering comfort to their confused minds. That five-hour drive home was the longest drive of my life.

Larry was concerned about my emotional state and kept reminding me, "Don't let Satan in, Kim." He knew Nicole's death had the potential to completely crush and destroy me. It was only a few short weeks prior I had boldly proclaimed to Larry there was no way that God would take one of our kids, because He wouldn't give me more than I could handle and I certainly couldn't handle that. What I came to realize is that I was right, I couldn't handle losing Nicole left to my own power. However, God promises to fill and strengthen me with His power. The Lord did just that, He picked me up and carried me.

- *Grief Note.* There is no right or wrong way to respond to seeing your loved one after they have passed away. Do what is right for you, trust God, trust your instinct. Whether a loss is expected or unexpected, it can be confusing and overwhelming, powerful and intimidating. Don't let someone make you do something you are uncomfortable with because it's what they would do or what they need.

- *Love Them Well.* Follow the lead of those who have experienced the devastating loss. If they need a hug, hold them tightly. If they need to not be touched, respect their space. If they want to cry, cry with them. If they want to pray, pray with them. Sit quietly and respectfully if your faith differs from theirs. If they want to scream, patiently let them.

Chapter 3:

Going Home

"Blessed are those who mourn,
for they will be comforted"
(Matthew 5:4).

A s we drove from the hospital, I vacillated between panic and disbelief. My mind was having a difficult time processing the events of the past several hours. Earlier that day, we had been enjoying breakfast together at McDonald's, discussing what type of ATV to rent and where to set up camp on the beach. How could we be driving home now without our girl?

The long drive home felt like a lifetime. The routine seemed so ludicrous to me, as the world outside continued to go on, as if nothing had happened. The ordinary things, such as getting gas in our truck or buying food, felt out of place in our world. Because of the drastic and sudden change in our lives, I felt the rest of the world should realize our pain and devastation. I wanted to scream out so everyone would know that the world was not the same. It would never be the same.

I know the Lord carried us those miles back to the town where we lived. I believe He dispatched His angels to surround us at that time, as He has done many days since. I'm so thankful for Larry's continuing prayer of "Don't let Satan in." I believe that prayer helped me remember I had a choice of where to look and whose hand to take. In my devastating heartbreak, I didn't have to let Satan have victory in our hearts and minds

Looking back, I believe I was in shock. All of us were. I'm so thankful God created our bodies in such a way that we can only take in so much. It is almost as if a fog of protection moves into our minds. Even still, my emotions were intensely close to despair. Larry knew I was dangerously close to being crushed in my pain. As he was driving, he would look at me often to check on me. He would pray out loud, asking the Lord to protect our minds and keep us from despair. Arlene would speak words of truth in the form of prayer and scripture. I do believe these things kept us from losing it completely. I should have been in a heap on the floor of the truck, but instead God scooped me up and helped me breathe each agonizing breath.

As we traveled along the dark highway, we had to make decisions about how to break this heartbreaking news to the many people who loved our girl. This proved to be one of the most agonizing parts of the whole process. It was hard enough to try to reconcile the loss of Nicole in our minds, but how were we to say it out loud? Not just one time, but over and over again, bracing ourselves for the reaction we would receive. We decided we would try to pray before each conversation because we needed God's divine intervention with each family member and friend.

I made Kevin (Nicole's boyfriend) call his parents as we drove to our home. He said he could drive himself back to his house, but I felt unsure about him driving alone after all that had taken place. His parents were there to meet us as we pulled into our driveway. They hugged us and wept with us as we shared the news. After they left to go home, we went next door to my parent's house. Walking through the door of their house in the middle of the night was one of many difficult doors we would have to walk through during the next few weeks.

Lisa was still awake in the living room and was startled to see us when we walked in the house. She had such a difficult time comprehending the terrible news she was hearing. She kept asking Larry over and over if he was joking. As I looked down the hall to my parent's bedroom, I knew I had to speak the words that would bring enormous pain into their lives; words no grandparent should ever have to hear. I remember walking through the door to their bedroom and wishing I could just allow them to continue sleeping peacefully. I knew once I woke them, their world would be forever changed. Nicole was my parents' first grandchild and held a special place in their hearts. There was no easy way to say the words, as their sleepy minds tried to understand why I was standing in their room. The word "devastating" doesn't even begin to describe those painful moments. Each time we told a new person Nicole had gone to Heaven, our souls ripped open a little more.

A family friend, Carol, and our youth pastor, Buzzy, showed up shortly after I told my parents. I don't remember calling either of them during the drive back, but I must have. Carol's and Buzzy's act of love, by showing up in the dark, early morning hour, brought comfort and strength. They didn't ask a lot of questions, they just listened to us. I can't remember many details of their visit, except they were present. And their hugs, tears and prayers gave us the comfort to know we would not be walking the road ahead of us alone. After our friends left, we knew we needed to get some sleep as the sun would be coming up soon, but we couldn't bring ourselves to go home. So, the five of us slept fitfully on the floor in my parent's living room, acutely aware of Nicole's absence.

It almost surprised me that the sun had the audacity to rise that morning. In the first few moments of my waking, I was confused. Why were the five of us sleeping on my parent's floor? I had to ask myself if it all had been a horrible dream. As reality slowly seeped in around the edges of my mind, so did the pain and disbelief of what had happened less than twenty-four hours earlier. As I lay there wishing desperately that it was not true, I had to will myself to stand up.

It would be the first day of many I would have to will myself to get up in the morning, to take on the day. We had some tremendously difficult tasks ahead of us. We had to call our friends and family to deliver the incomprehensible news that Nicole had gone to Heaven. We did pray before most of those phone calls and I believe that the Lord covered those calls. As a matter of fact, as our courage waned, we had to pray often, fervently asking the Lord to keep us from despair.

The first week was a blur as we tried to gain our footing on the constantly shifting ground below us. Just when we would begin to feel steady, another wave of pain would hit us and remind us of the reality of Nicole's death. There were arrangements to be made and the enormity of the tasks at hand were overwhelming. We had to plan Nicole's memorial service and wanted to make it one that would honor her memory and glorify God. We filled our days with preparations for her service as we looked through pictures and watched videos that captured just a glimpse of her life. In some ways, it was a sweet time as we reminisced with the friends and family who filled the house with love, cards and casseroles.

However, being winter, the days were short and as the sun began to sink low, so did my heart. The darkness outside seemed to mirror the darkness I felt in my soul. I struggled immensely in the evening and nighttime to keep from going into despair. I had to continually fight to give God my pain. In this, I learned when you surrender something to the Lord, it is not a one-time offering. Rather, I had to give Him my despair, my pain, my sorrow, and my anger repeatedly.

We still could not stand the thought of going home to stay, so we stayed at my parents' house for a time. Our house was a reminder of life with our family of six, who now was a family of five. Walking through the door of our home would scream the brutal reality of the unfinished projects, unfinished dreams and, to our minds, an unfinished life. If we needed anything, we would rush next door to our house, do what we had to do, and get out of there fast.

Every day, the sun would continue to rise. And every day, I awoke and tried to process the events of the past week. Every day precious people would show up to love us and support us. Some loved on us in tangible yet subtle ways, arriving, doing what needed doing, and leaving without me even seeing them or being aware of their visit. Friends, acquaintances and loved ones would fill the fridge with food and bottled water and clean up messes that needed to be cleaned. Some of our 4-H and horse show friends perceived our need, showing up to feed and water the animals. They then went above and beyond by cleaning the stalls. They didn't know what to say, but they came.

What do you say to a devastated, grieving family? The truth is, there is often nothing to be said, no magical words that will make it all better. But the actions and care of the community acted as a salve to our wounded hearts. Some of the greatest comfort we received came from those who said little, but just showed up. People from our church, from our school and community came to cry with us and hold us. The cards and flowers were symbols of their love and support for us. I didn't always read the cards right then, but I cherished them in the weeks to come, when the visitors began to thin out and I felt alone.

Often, I didn't know what I needed and would just lay on the living room floor. I remember specifically one day, I was laying on the floor, drowning in my sadness and felt like I couldn't possibly get up, when someone came in. I can't remember who it was, but they sat on the floor next to me and I put my head in their lap. Whoever it was just stroked my head, they didn't say anything, but just that simple act of love was like balm on my brokenness. Those are the acts of love that really stand out to me as I remember the kindness of people. The ones who expected nothing from us in return. They loved us without expectations or judgement.

If you are a friend of someone who has lost a loved one, especially a child, just show up. Don't worry if you feel like you don't have all the right words. You're right, you don't. Because there are no words that can ease their pain. No platitudes of comfort that will fix their broken hearts. Grief isn't a disease to be healed or fixed. So please don't feel discouraged if your words of comfort don't seem to bring comfort. In all likelihood, those words will come back to them later and will bring a measure of peace. We all grieve in different ways. There is no right or wrong way to handle sorrow. Your presence is what matters.

Remember, they may not be able to acknowledge your presence or even be aware of you being there. That is why cards and notes were such a huge help to me. I did not always remember or even know that someone was there. But there was always a stack of cards on the table. When the loneliness descended, I would read them and remember I wasn't alone. I knew there were many people I could call at the drop of a hat and they would be right there.

Especially during the shock of the first few weeks, just show up and don't be afraid to do something that obviously needs to be done. Taking out the trash, wiping off the counters or even cleaning the bathroom. My friend Marci knew our Christmas decorations were still strewn all over our house. I had mentioned to her that I dreaded taking down and packing them away. Marci asked me if it would be helpful for her to take them down for me, so I wouldn't have to face that task. I gratefully told her yes. She gathered some other friends and bought some crates and lovingly packed everything away neatly. They labeled all the crates and put them in our storage container, so we had one less thing to worry about. I was glad she asked if it would be helpful and she was very respectful of our wishes. She was careful to ask if there was any special way I wanted to handle the decorations or store them. She taught me to be brave enough to see a need and ask permission to help with that need.

If there is any doubt about moving an item, doing something or throwing something away, ask your friend or just leave it. For instance, after my mother-in-law went to be with Jesus, her shoes were left under the coffee table, right where she left them. No one said anything about it, but it was just unspoken, no one touched the shoes. The placement of her shoes was almost sacred and it was up to my father-in-law to decide if and when to move them, when he felt ready.

The simple acts of kindness, not requiring a response, yet just being there, meant the world to us. Our friends did all that for us and we will never be able to acknowledge all of what they did. Those selfless souls that attended to our needs brought comfort in ways I could never repay, but for which I am so very thankful. Romans 12 admonishes us to "be devoted to one another in love. Honor one another above yourselves" (v. 10). It goes on to say, "Be joyful in hope, patient in affliction, faithful in prayer. Share with the Lord's people who are in need. Practice hospitality" (v. 12–13). These friends and acquaintances truly walked this biblical principle out. They mourned with us as we mourned, they practiced hospitality, they were devoted to us. They blessed us beyond all measure.

My friend Terri wrote this about her experience with people caring for her after her daughter Heather went to Heaven. "Amazing women from a church we weren't even members of would descend upon our home when we weren't there and bring food and supplies. We never saw most of them, they just knew how to do God's work. I can never, ever repay the kindness and love shown to us on those difficult days. That kind of love can only be paid forward. I pray that when God calls upon my heart to do so, I am enough. The love of those women and all of Heather's friends during that time sustained us".

The Lord propped up our broken hearts as we shared the news of Nicole's death with people who dearly loved her. He gave us the courage to face each difficult door through which we had to walk. I'm so thankful we didn't have to go home all at once. I'm even more grateful we were surrounded by amazing people who supported us through many of the difficult decisions that needed to be made as we planned her memorial service. Walking through the door to the funeral home was the hardest walk of all.

- *Grief Note.* If you feel in shock, in disbelief, or in a fog, especially at the beginning, it's okay. It's God's way of protecting our hearts and minds from shattering under the weight and magnitude of what has transpired. You will wade out of the fog in due time. Take it little by little.

- *Grief Note.* Grief is not a one-time thing. Rather, it comes in waves. At first, the waves come hard and fast. Eventually, there is space between the waves. You may have moments of peace and even joy. Another wave does not mean you are failing in your grief. Hang in there as the tides of grief ebb and flow.

- *Love Them Well.* Show up. If you see a need, meet it. Ask for permission but be specific. "Let me know if you need anything" is too vague. Someone grieving doesn't necessarily know what they need. Saying, "Would you like me to mow, vacuum, bring food, take the kids, etc." is specific but still allows your loved one to provide guidance as to what they need. Use the giftings God has instilled in you, whatever it is.

- *Love Them Well.* Keep in mind long visits can be hard. Be cognizant of your hurting friend's needs and emotions. Remember that a person who has just suffered the dramatic loss of a loved one is extremely raw. It is as if their very nerves are on the surface of their skin and may be hypersensitive. Be careful to observe their emotional condition and be sensitive to what they need.

Chapter 4:

The Service

"For I am convinced that neither death nor life...will
be able to separate us from the love of God that is in
Christ Jesus our Lord"
(Romans 8:38–39).

We found solace while we were planning Nicole's memorial service. It gave us a purpose and we were determined to make it a day to honor her memory and celebrate her life. We poured over pictures to fill the videos and poster boards to display at the service. Every photo we looked at represented a memory of Nicole and the fun times our family enjoyed together. To choose a limited number of photos felt impossible, because we wanted everyone at the service to be able to share those memories with us. The tech guys at our church were so patient as we stretched the limit of photos and the video length continually.

Music is an extremely powerful motivator and we found much encouragement as we listened to the songs Nicole loved. Hearing her music inspired us to be strong and reminded us of her. Like the photos, certain songs would usher in a fun memory. One song could instantly take us back to a concert where Nicole, with multiple braids in her hair, was having fun, freely dancing to the music. She had a way of getting everyone else on board, braids and all.

It was a bittersweet time as we attempted to sum up Nicole's life into a one-hour service. She had lived so many lifetimes in her short seventeen years and touched so many people's lives. There were many tears while we laboriously went through every detail, as we attempted to soak in every ounce of her existence. Those were the more therapeutic tasks we had to complete for Nicole's memorial service. But then there were the simply painful ones. Going to the mortuary and cemetery were by far the most difficult.

We were no strangers to cemeteries. My dad was the grounds superintendent for our local cemetery and we owned a cemetery service construction company. We worked at the very cemetery in which Nicole's body was to be buried. Despite our familiarity with cemeteries, we were so blessed to have our friend Carol come along to help us with the arrangements. We had experience on the construction side of the fence. Suddenly, we were on the grieving parent's side of the fence.

As we approached, I could not fathom walking through those doors. I knew once we walked through those doors I had to choose a casket for my sweet girl. Her body would go into the ground. I sure didn't feel the least bit brave at that point, but I had to get brave. In my mind I had to do it for Nicole. I had to honor her in a special way.

Everyone has individual ways to deal with the difficult steps when you lay a loved one to rest. The staff in the mortuary are trained to walk hurting families through those steps, which is helpful. However, they were sales people who didn't have a deep knowledge of who Nicole was or who we were as a family. Consequently, we found it necessary to stand firm on some of the details of Nicole's burial. We had unique, non-traditional components we wanted to include, which were meaningful to our family. So, if you are currently walking through this part of your journey, please don't feel pressure to conform to traditions that don't fit your family.

Some choose to have donations sent to a charity in lieu of flowers or to release doves as a representation of the spirit's release to Heaven. For us, we chose to honor Nicole with flowers and I cherished each arrangement that was sent to us. Every flower represented beautiful life and I needed that. Do whatever brings comfort to you and your family and honors your loved one.

The mortuary staff person greeted us as we finally got up the strength to walk into the waiting room of the mortuary. She took us to a room where we discussed what our expectations were for Nicole's service and burial. She was kind as she walked us through the decisions we would need to make and guided us in to the room that held the caskets.

It felt odd to go into a room whose only purpose was to display a variety of caskets. There were simple options and there were extravagant options, but for me, it felt like an alternate reality in which I didn't belong. As we walked around the room taking in our choices, I was so torn. How do parents choose a casket in which to bury their child? It seemed so absurd. We ultimately decided on a simple wooden casket for Nicole that seemed to fit her unpretentious spirit. I wanted flowers that represented her simple beauty, so we chose a white spray of flowers to rest on top of her casket. After making those hard choices, we walked out with the sales person to choose a plot of ground that would ultimately be the resting place for Nicole's earthly body. We decided on a plot under a tree near the area where my parents would eventually be buried. We ended up buying three plots total because at the time, we thought it would important to have any of us who passed away to be buried there near her.

The plots that we purchased were undeveloped, meaning that they didn't have the concrete boxes called lawn crypts already in place. The lawn crypts hold the casket. Because of our connections with the cemetery, they allowed Larry, his dad and his brother-in-law Will to install the lawn crypts. That was an honor for Larry and he felt like it was his place as Nicole's dad to be able to do that for her.

There are so many things that you don't think about having to do until you are put in the position of planning a funeral for a loved one. There seemed to be a myriad of decisions we had to make from flowers and clothes she would wear, to the writing of the obituary.

When it came to writing an obituary, I was at a loss. I really struggled to put in words a description that would honor Nicole's memory and describe the amazing person she is. Thankfully our friend Susie came to the rescue. We had met Susie when we bought Nicole's first show horse Coco. She became Nicole's trainer and our family friend. Susie and Nicole spent countless hours together riding and talking. Nicole loved her dearly. Susie sat by my side, in front of my computer and helped me write the words that would be printed in the newspaper announcing the news of Nicole's death. I can never thank her enough for the gift she gave me that day.

When the mortuary asked us to bring in some clothes in which to dress Nicole, I wondered how I would look through her clothes to decide what to take. I don't even really remember the process of looking, but I do remember what we picked out. Nicole didn't usually wear dressy clothes, she had a natural, casual kind of beauty. She was more comfortable in jeans and t-shirts, with her hair in a messy bun. However, she had recently had her senior pictures taken, so we decided on one of the outfits she had worn for that. I gingerly placed her black dress pants, and white button up blouse in a bag, along with her barely worn dress shoes, and took them to the mortuary.

We chose not to have an open casket for the visitation or the service, but we wanted to allow the immediate family members an opportunity to see her if they felt like it was something they wanted to do. So, we had some time before the open visitation for that purpose. I still didn't feel compelled to see her in the casket. I felt strongly in my spirit I had to remember her alive and thriving. I was struggling enough with the memories of her accident and I wanted to establish in my mind her wild, free life. Nonetheless, we wanted each person to be able to grieve in their own way, the way that best suited their hearts.

Again, I have trouble remembering certain events clearly. It's like certain parts of my memory have been snatched away, never to be recovered, only experienced in feelings or snapshots. The first snapshot I remember of the memorial service is us walking into the back of the chapel for the visitation and seeing Nicole's casket surrounded by beautiful flowers. I wanted to read each card on the flowers and soak in the love expressed there. My heart was like a cavern and I craved goodness, beauty and love.

So many people came that night, but I couldn't really describe it in detail. A few, however, are etched in my mind. The sad, desperate expression on some faces, not able to comprehend the absolute loss they were feeling. I was overwhelmed with the outpouring of love for our family. We saw many people we never expected to see. Those from far away, from business connections and some we hadn't seen for years. There is a commonality in death that brings people together. We are all born and we all die. Death will eventually touch all of us and that fact connects people in a special way.

The next day as we prepared to go to the memorial, I struggled with the basic decision of what to wear. No one ever plans to pick out an appropriate outfit to wear to their child's memorial service. I just knew I didn't want to wear black. Black represented death to me and I wanted to celebrate her life. But I also felt like bright colors did not represent what was going on in my soul, so I chose a gray skirt.

Our youth pastor, Buzzy, was very protective of us that day and waited to bring us in until most of the people were seated. As we walked down the center aisle of our church's gym, my eyes went forward to the stage. There, perfectly centered in front of the stage was that simple wooden casket with the white flowers draped over it. I became acutely aware of the fact that Nicole's earthly body lay in that casket. She was wearing the black dress pants and white button up white blouse. I forced myself to remember that even though her body lay in that casket, she was not in there. Her physical life on earth was over, but we believe with all our hearts and minds that she lives in Heaven. That was an overriding thought from which I drew great comfort in those days. I believe Nicole was then and is still more alive than I am and in the presence of God. I don't think our earthly minds can comprehend completely about Heaven, but I do believe with all that I am, this earth is not all there is.

It was time to start the service and our pastor came to us and said there was still a long line to get into the church gym. He wanted to shelter us from more pain and was worried about the delay. We assured him we were fine and to please wait and let all the people come in. The gym was full and soon became standing room only with people who loved Nicole. The sheer number of people in attendance amazed and humbled us. It was as if Nicole herself had compelled a gathering to celebrate life. When our pastor Tom Mercer came to the stage, he said, "Nicole invited 800 people to church today." All walks of life, young and old, some we had never met or never will. Nicole had brought us together and, in some ways, connected us for a lifetime. Through the songs and speaking, our hearts were knitted together.

The band consisted of the music leaders and youth group band. One of my dear friends sang "It is Well with My Soul." My mom was drowning in her pain and requested we sing a song she and Nicole had sung. "Thank you, Lord for saving my soul; thank you, Lord for making me whole; thank you, Lord for giving to me; thy great salvation so rich and free"

Lisa courageously spoke from her heart about Nicole. As we all participated in the service, it felt like we were a part of eternity. It was almost as if I could hear Nicole participate on the other side of a curtain that separated us from Heaven. When the service was over, the pall bearers came forward to wheel her casket up the aisle to the awaiting hearse. Our family stood to follow her casket and I remember catching the eyes of so many of our dear friends. I saw love, sympathy and encouragement in their eyes.

I don't remember getting in the truck or arriving at the cemetery for the graveside service, but I do have a vivid snap shot of Nicole's casket being tenderly carried away from the hearse. I can see the broken-hearted young men in dress clothes and older men in suits carrying the simple casket with their beloved Nicole in it. Heads bowed in grief as they honored her well in their hearts. It is more than I can stand to think about, even all these years later. We had more songs, some of her friends spoke and it was over.

For some, the day of the service may not bring comfort. It may just seem like an ordeal that solidifies the pain in their hearts. Also, being with a large crowd of people during grief may only cause stress and anxiety for others. It is important that you give yourself room to grieve in the way that brings the most comfort. Please do not judge yourself by anyone else's experiences or opinions. Don't allow anyone to tell you how to feel. If a small private graveside is all you feel like you can emotionally handle, then that is what you should do. Maybe for some, it is cremation and scattering of your loved one's ashes in a special, meaningful place. Every situation is different and every person reacts in a variety of ways.

For me, the day brought comfort and I didn't want it to end. Our friends and family lingered after the service had concluded. I'm so glad they did. People who hadn't seen each other in years hugged and caught up with one another. Wispy white clouds stood out in the bright blue sky on that unusually warm January day. It was a special, sacred happening and I didn't want people to leave. When they left, it would be real and I wasn't ready to face reality.

- *Grief Note.* Have the courage and confidence to stand firm on what will make the service lovely and appropriate to honor your loved one. Sales people at a mortuary do not know them. You do. Personalize the service as best suits you, your family and your loved one.

- *Grief Note.* Its okay to not remember every detail of the service. Some people find themselves still in shock, operating in survival mode. Having a video montage of photos and music may be soothing and comforting in the aftermath. You may remember it later in small memories or flashes.
- *Grief Note.* Cherish the cards you receive at the service. Keep a small piece of some of the arrangements if it brings you comfort. But also, don't be afraid to request other ways to honor your loved one's life, such as donations.
- *Love Them Well.* Respect the wishes set forth by the family. If they request a specific attire (no black, wearing a favorite color, sports paraphernalia) adhere to it if possible.
- *Love Them Well.* Your presence at the visitation or service is meaningful, even if the family is unable to spend time with you at the service. Be mindful of their needs. If the graveside service is private, don't intrude. If they are comforted by the companionship, continue to visit.

Chapter 5:

Reality Sets In

*"I will be with you; I will never leave you nor forsake
you. Be strong and courageous"*
(Joshua 1:5b–6a).

In the days following the accident, we spent so much time
preparing for the service, we didn't know what to do with
ourselves when it was over.

The crowd began to thin as people walked to their cars to go
back to their own homes and families. There were hugs and tears
and promises of future get-togethers. As each person walked
away from the cemetery that day, the reality of life without Nicole
began to set in. We were so immersed in taking care of the details
of planning her service and the determination to make it a joyful
day, we hadn't given much consideration to the painful task of
just living our day-to-day lives.

The five of us walked away from the grave that was to hold Nicole's earthly body and walked into the new reality of our life without her. We climbed in our truck and knew we needed the comfort of something familiar. So, we collectively decided we should go to In-N-Out Burger. We went through the drive-through and placed our usual order, that is, our usual order minus one. I believe we chose In-N-Out because we were craving something ordinary from our old lives. That is the thing about facing our new reality after such a traumatic event, we just ached for something we knew. In-N-Out was not significant for any reason, except that we went there often, especially when we were working on a project around the house. As we stepped into our future, we longed to pull the comfort of our past with us. We ate our burgers in the truck and began to consider what was next for our family.

As we drove back after dinner, we discussed and realized what was next. We knew we needed to eventually leave the sanctuary of my parents' house and learn how to live in our own home again, but we weren't ready yet. I don't remember how long it took for us to finally go home after Nicole's service. But when we did it was like pushing our family through to another dimension. A place where life with Nicole had once existed, but we could no longer touch her or see her.

It was January and it felt bitterly cold to me, both outside and inside our home. We used a wood burning stove for our heat and the stove hadn't had a fire kindled in it for quite some time. Building a fire was the first task Larry tackled to try to bring us warmth. Warmth seemed to elude me in those days and I felt a constant chill. It seemed the bleak winter season outside had taken over my soul. I craved sunshine. I guess I thought if I could just sit and soak the sun into my body, it would warm and fill the spot where grief had come to reside.

As the days dragged on, we felt a series of vicious emotional assaults, as the reality of life without Nicole slammed us repeatedly. We felt as though we had been thrown into the old children's game, Barrel of Monkeys. We were shaken furiously before being dumped out on the ground in a jumbled heap. The rest of the world still turned, still functioned, still continued on like before. But for me, the new reality lacked color and order. As we began to untangle ourselves from one another, we had to step into a world that looked familiar but was not the same.

The house that was once a home of six now only held five. Everywhere I looked in the house held a memory and a piece of Nicole: Horse Show entry forms she planned to complete when she returned from our Pismo trip; clothes discarded on the floor that she chose not to pack; Christmas gifts she was so grateful to receive. We didn't move her unfinished projects, for fear of erasing the memory of her. I would lay in her bed and press her clothes to my face in the attempt to soak her scent into me. It was like being next to her for a moment as I closed my eyes and breathed in. We would listen to the messages she had left on the answering machine, so we could hear her sweet, cheerful voice. Everywhere we looked, listened or smelled was a reminder of her. All our senses perceived she was there, but she was not.

The barn was another bittersweet place that held countless memories. Nicole spent many hours in the barnyard with the horses. After she left for Heaven, even the simplest tasks like feeding animals and cleaning stalls took on a whole new meaning. Projects Nicole had begun in the tack room lay unfinished. Her horse Coco and dog Nala seemed to grasp that something was very different and appeared to be grieving as well.

I had the intense longing to see, hold and touch Nicole. I felt as if I should just be able to pick up the phone and call her. Facing the reality that she was not there and I could not see, hold or touch her pressed in on me, threatening to crush my soul. Practically every day for the past seventeen years, I saw her sweet face and talked to her. Every day, I had heard her call me "Mama" and felt her give me hugs.

Sorrow is not something you can lay aside for a while. It's not a burden you can put down to get a break when it becomes too heavy. It clings on you and invades every part of your existence. It was difficult for me to prevent grief from defining who I was. I had to work hard not to identify myself as Kim, the one who lost her daughter, Nicole. Instead I fought to continue to be Larry's wife, mom to Lisa, Megan and Alex, and most of all, Kim, whom God loves. Kim, for whom God still had a purpose, instead of a shell of a person who only housed pain and grief.

I'm so thankful the shock the Lord allowed us to experience as a measure of protection didn't wear off all at once. Moments of realization would come sporadically, and sink into my mind, so I would be able to make sense of all of it. Some of those moments came crashing in unexpectedly, vehemently reminding me Nicole was no longer with us on earth. Other times, they would ease in and just settle with a sadness that felt like it would never leave.

Seemingly trivial truths, like her being the only one of the Peacock kids who were able to drive yet, snuck up as painful reminders. When we were rushed or didn't feel like cooking, Nicole was always the one to make a Baja Burrito run. Now there was no one to drive and run errands. Her bright purple truck just sat there in the driveway empty, like a precious relic from happier days.

Though our world and lives felt upheaved, Larry had to go back to work and the kids had to go back to school. Bills had to be paid. It is interesting to think back on all the things I thought were so important before Nicole went to Heaven and that I allowed to stress me out. Death brings clarity to our lives, if we allow it. It shows us what is important to keep on the "To Do" list and what can be let go.

Unfortunately, there were also painful tasks to complete. The three-wheeler Nicole was riding at the time of her accident was still at the Ranger's station in Oceano Dunes. Because it was an accident, an investigation was required to ensure nothing was amiss that may have contributed to it. Once that was completed and everything came back clear, we had to decide what to do with the three-wheeler. The ATV was the epitome and representation of everything evil that had stolen my girl. We never wanted to think about it or even lay eyes on it again.

We decided it would be best to just give it to the ranger station. We just wanted to be rid of it and make it cease to exist. That should be easy enough, right? No, it wasn't. There were endless phone calls, talking about it, explaining the situation repeatedly, painfully. Paperwork had to be filled out before we could just be liberated from the piece of metal that I wished I could just make disappear from the earth. The harsh reality was the inanimate object that took our very lively Nicole from us was still here while she wasn't. It made me extremely angry. It was hard enough just waking up without Nicole every day, having to deal with the Ranger's Station just felt cruel. It wasn't the rangers' faults. They were just doing their jobs. I just didn't want to deal with it.

And just as one painful task would end, another would rear its ugly head. As we jumbled monkeys fought to untangle, reality settled in. It wasn't that everything we had to do was as painfully sharp as ridding ourselves of the ATV. It was just that every day we had to learn to do life without her. The oozing wound of grief infected everything we did. While I watched the rest of the world continue on, I felt it was impossible for life to continue. If someone told me I would have thirty or forty more years in front of me, I would have screamed at the impossibility of it. Time would not, could not continue. But it did. Morning after morning, the sun would rise and time would continue. I would read quotes and verses like Proverbs 31:25, "She is clothed with strength and dignity; she can laugh at the days to come." And Jeremiah 29:11, "'For I know the plans I have for you [Kim],' declares the Lord, ... 'plans to give you a hope and a future.'"

Those verses did bring me comfort eventually, but during those first extremely hard days, I just couldn't see a future. I really was convinced the world was going to end soon and Jesus had to be coming back any day to take us from the earth. The idea of laughing at the days to come or a plan and future for my life eluded me. I had to fight from being void of hope.

As I battled my darkness, I learned about the "standard" stages of grief: Denial, Anger, Bargaining, Depression, Acceptance. These are not the only correct ways to grieve. If you do not experience each one in this particular order, it doesn't mean you aren't grieving in the correct fashion. I went to a therapist because I was concerned I was not grieving properly. She was quick to assure me there is no correct or incorrect way to grieve. But there are tools and techniques that can help us as we go through the process. I have experienced components of all the stages of grief, but not necessarily in order or in full. However, I do believe Denial accurately describes what I was going through during what I would call the "reality sets in" season.

I just was not able to grasp the concept of life without Nicole at first and it was painful. However, every day the Lord would pick me up and carry me through what I thought was impossible.

He would show me glimpses of hope in the darkness of the firsts of life without Nicole. My friend Ilene said it this way when describing making it through a particularly difficult time in her life, "Every day you just get up and put your shoes on." Or as Tom Hanks' character, Sam Baldwin so aptly said in *Sleepless in Seattle*, "Well, I'm going to get out of bed every morning, breathe in and out all day long. Then after a while, I won't have to remind myself to get out of bed every morning and breathe in and out." You know what? They're right. Walking through every moment of every day felt impossible. But God showed us that every day, He made the impossible, possible. He truly did have a plan for a hope and a future for us, even if we couldn't see it at the time.

God showed us ways of doing life without Nicole. As we untangled ourselves, it was like a toddler learning to walk. Sometimes falling. Sometimes falling hard. But again and again, the Lord would pick us up.

There is no easy, ten-step formula to survive those days unscathed. However, there are some things I learned to do in order to cope with the intense, sharp pain of those first days.

I had to learn to let go of my, or anyone else's, expectations of what my grief should look like. Each person's grief is theirs alone. I discovered that Larry and I grieved differently from each other, as did the kids. Our grief journeys were mostly parallel with one another. But they didn't necessarily cross, nor did we experience the same thing at the same time. Rather, as in many aspects of our life together, we walked our grief journeys side by side. It was important to give each other space to feel our own individual emotions without judging the validity of one another's grief.

Because Larry was the first one to get to Nicole and saw her injuries up close, because he gave her CPR, it was important to him to be able to talk about some of the details that had happened. We discussed it and together both felt it would be damaging to my heart to hear some of the details that he needed to be able to discuss. To protect my mind, we decided he would not talk about those events with me. He needed to talk to someone else about the images that he was struggling with. He talked to our youth pastor Buzzy and my brother-in-law, George, about those things. That was extremely helpful for him. It was hardest for us to talk to the ones closest to us about some of the specific ways we were struggling in our grief. We were blessed to have someone explain early on that it was perfectly normal to feel this way. We desperately didn't want to be misunderstood. While Larry had people he confided in, I had other people in whom I felt safe to confide. I had women who walked close to me during that time. But it was also helpful for me to see a Christian therapist to work through some of the intense feelings with which I struggled.

I was blessed because both my friends and therapist would direct me to scripture for a constant source of truth. I couldn't trust my own emotions or thoughts sometimes, but the Bible was my anchor. It was also a bridge from my hurting soul to eternity. It helped me remember Nicole was vibrant and alive in Heaven. Heaven wasn't some mythical place beyond reality. Heaven is real and the Lord pressed on my heart in a heavy way that I needed to stay connected to Him and His word for my survival. It was vital for us to incorporate scripture in everything we did, especially when it came time for choosing Nicole's headstone. It took us a while to make a final decision on it, because it would literally be etched in stone and we wanted it to be perfect. We talked to the family and Lisa mentioned Joshua 1:9. It was significant to her because it was the theme verse from a mission trip on which she and Nicole had gone.

Joshua 1:9 says, "Have I not commanded you? Be strong and courageous. Do not be afraid; do not be discouraged, for the Lord your God will be with you wherever you go."

That verse was powerful to us as we faced our new reality. The first chapter of Joshua talks about Joshua's new reality. Moses, his leader, had died and Joshua was now in charge of getting the Israelites across the Jordan river into the Promise Land. He must have been scared to death, because the words "Be strong and courageous" are repeated four times in this short chapter! Joshua was told to keep the Book of the Law always on his lips, meditating on it day and night. This speaks volumes to me as I reflect on those first few weeks and months after Nicole died. I don't know if I realized it then, but while the Bible brought me comfort, holding onto it helped me have courage. I didn't not feel courageous, but God's words were a command to me, to BE STRONG AND COURAGEOUS, reminding me that He was with me. The word BE implies that I had a choice to be brave. I do believe being courageous wasn't in my own power, but by yielding to God's power, He caused me to have courage. Facing my heartbreak victoriously would require that I be intentional about being brave. Brave doesn't just happen.

- *Grief Note.* Allow old, familiar places, things and routines to bring small measures of comfort to the upheaval.
- *Grief Note.* Give grace to yourself and your family members to grieve the way YOU need. It will not be the same for each of you. You each had a unique relationship with your loved one who has gone to Heaven. And God put unique personalities and needs in each of you.
- *Love Them Well.* Speak truth in love, as God leads. Do not be offended or feel slighted if the comfort you intend is not received as you expect in the beginning. The

grievers are getting their bearings. But the words you share from God will come back to their minds and hearts when they are most needed.

- *Love Them Well.* Be willing to be still, to listen, with the griever. Let them pour out their hearts and hurts. You may be the safe space they need in order to heal, while still protecting their other family members

Chapter 6:

Contagious Courage

"Two are better than one, because they have a good return for their labor; If either of them falls down, one can help the other up. But pity anyone who falls and has no one to help them up"
(Ecclesiastes 4:9–12).

When my courage would begin to wear thin and I thought I couldn't take another step, the Lord sent people into my path to encourage me. Incredibly, it would be just what I needed at the precise moment I needed it. (Isn't God kind and wonderful that way?!)

Maybe it was a phone call or a note in the mail, but help always came. I had to watch for it sometimes, because in my defeated state, I could miss the provisions God bestowed. The Bible encourages us to be ever-watchful. When I would keep my eyes searching for the Lord, He never failed to be my ever-present help in time of need.

My friend Nellie would periodically send letters in the mail and just wrote down what she felt the Lord was prompting her to write. Her words were always the exact nourishment my soul needed. One day I felt alone and felt as if no one else understood my grief. As I sat in my office, I was immersed in a pity party of epic proportions and convinced the rest of the world had gone ahead, leaving me and Nicole's memory behind.

As I grudgingly thumbed through the mail on my desk, a familiar blue envelope and welcoming handwriting jumped out at me from among the sea of mundane envelopes. It was the stationary that my friend Nellie always used to send me encouragement. Like a starving person, I tore into the envelope to devour the words my friend wrote.

Again, it was just what I needed. She wrote about how she noticed the pretty wispy clouds in the sky that day, like the clouds that were in the sky the day of Nicole's service. She said she was reminded of Nicole and shared some memories with me. What a gift!

I told Nellie what her letters meant to me and she seemed genuinely surprised. She stated she didn't feel like she said anything profound. She just listened to the Lord's prompting and wrote what was on her heart. I've saved each of the letters she sent me and have drawn encouragement every time I've reread them.

That is just one example of how God would send champions of faith to inspire me and give me courage to take another step.

After Nicole's passing, I was incredibly drawn to other people who had lost children. Broken hearts bind us together in unimaginable ways that bring comfort. I felt like there was no way we could survive the anguish we were experiencing, but when I saw other people who had survived a similar loss, I felt a connection. It was as if suddenly we were part of a secret club. It is a club no one chooses to join, but we were so very thankful for it nonetheless.

On the evening of the visitation prior to Nicole's memorial service, a man walked in that we had never met. After he told us his name, he said he had heard about Nicole's accident and was compelled to come. His daughter Amanda had been hit and killed while crossing the road in front of her high school. He told us he felt a connection to us and wanted to assure us we were not alone. He told us we would make it through this and it would be okay. I remember looking intently at him, surprised that he was surviving, much less still a functioning person.

It took courage for him to walk into a visitation with people he had never met and share his heart. He was part of the club in which he didn't want to belong, but wanted us to know we were not walking this road alone. He was just one example of the brave ones who just came, wrote letters and sent cards of encouragement.

Now when I hear about someone who has lost a child, I feel compelled to seek them out. Many friendships have been forged through our common bonds. Some have very hard stories that leave chasms in their hearts which can never be completely crossed. Those of us in this club walk a diverse road, handling our loss in different ways, yet we all have one thing in common: we've lost a part ourselves when we lost our child. Their stories have helped me find my bearings and have given me the courage to keep pursuing a Victorious Heart.

Not too long ago I was at a cemetery in California and met a woman who was grieving over her daughter. She has visited the grave of her daughter every day for the last eight years.

Every day she brings a pillow and sits next to a headstone that has her daughter's name etched in stone. Every day she adjusts the beautiful decorations she so lovingly spreads over the plot of ground. Every day she grieves. I approached her to introduce myself and to tell her that I too, had lost my girl. I noticed by looking at her daughter's headstone that her and Nicole were both born on May 22. I explained our daughters shared a birthday. Despite the language barrier that was obvious to both of us, we instantly bonded. Our grief was our bond.

That day, in the midst of the bustle of a busy cemetery, time stood still. The noises of the nearby construction site faded away as I shared tears with this dedicated, loving mama. We held on to one another and wept for our daughters who shared a birthday. Through a connection that defied distance, culture or language barriers, our hearts were knitted together. As I walked away from her, I couldn't help but feel closer to Heaven and couldn't deny our meeting was divinely appointed. Who knows if our girls weren't up in Heaven together bonding themselves?

I was reminded of those sweet souls who I've met who are in this club. The faces and stories are fresh in my mind. They are courageous warriors who have walked victoriously in the broken places. Knowing them gives me courage and brings me comfort.

We are drawn to those who have faced heartache in the same areas we have experienced. Frequently, it is in those relationships that we find the strength we need to continue walking the difficult roads before us. Together, our lives sing a song that is birthed out of our painful circumstances. However, because of our own unique personal history, each one of us has a special chord which can only be sung by us individually. Some chords are born from the deepest wound, but when sung are beautiful and reach down to the center of the soul.

When I think of that deep chord, I think of my friend Denise. I knew Denise's daughter Holly, before I knew her. Holly had an infectious smile and a kind heart. She was one of the students in my High School small group. In a heated, emotionally charged moment Holly chose to take her own life. Cutting deeper still, it was in the presence of her brother and her mom Denise. The first time I met Denise was in the hospital waiting room after they had given the family the news that Holly hadn't made it. This was not even a year after Nicole went to Heaven and the wound of death was so fresh. But it was one of those moments, I was compelled to go. As you can imagine, Denise was in shock and numb. Over the next few months, Denise came to the Bible study group I led. She was resistant and struggling with bitterness. Who can blame her? You can't really measure or compare grief, but her loss was great and tragic.

Over the years I've known Denise, she has softened her heart and made a choice to live a life of intentional joy. If you saw Denise today, you would see shining eyes of hope and an infectious smile, like her girl Holly. You would see a positive, uplifting woman who has a passion for others and a desire to serve. You may not know that she is struggling with cancer right now, for the second time. You wouldn't know the depths of her heartache. At one time bitterness and anger threatened to overtake her, but she fought courageously to choose to give her pain to God. Amazingly, she has laid down her sorrow before God again and again.

Because of that, her life is a stunning song that brings harmony and hope to so many people. In her darkest days, God has produced a melody only Denise could sing. Denise is one of the bravest women I know, and I count it a privilege to be a witness to the song of her life.

Mrs. Charles Cowman (1997) says it beautifully:
> In the darkest night He is composing your song.
> In the valley, He is tuning your voice.
> In the storm clouds He is deepening your range.
> In the rain showers He is sweetening your melody.
> In the cold He is giving your notes expression.
> And as you pass at times from hope to fear,
> He is perfecting the message of your lyrics.

You have a song of healing and beauty. It is uniquely yours and combined with the songs of others, it produces a wonderful symphony. I am honored to be a witness of those melodies that strung together create a harmonious composition of life.

There has been another set of stories that have been a balm to the wound in my heart. Those are the stories of Nicole's life. The memories I have now take on new meaning, almost as if I am now learning lessons from the life she lived then.

We were given an album filled with notes from Nicole's friends. Some were from people I had never met, some were anonymous, and some were from people we had known for years. The pages contained memories of Nicole, how she touched their lives and lessons learned from her. It was a priceless gift that gave me an outside glimpse of her life from her friends' perspectives.

I don't know how she managed to accomplish so much in her short life. The day of her service, the gym at the church was packed to overflowing with people standing in line outside waiting to get in, many I had never met. Her life and then her death created a special event that drew so many together. One of our relatives marveled that while he was at the graveside service and struggling, some spiky-haired kid approached him, grabbing him on the shoulder to comfort him.

I love hearing all the stories, like the girl who had not fit in at youth group. She told me that no one accepted her because she didn't look like the typical "youth group" teen. Her pink hair and piercings had made some of the regulars feel uncomfortable, but not Nicole. The girl was in the foyer at the church and Nicole noticed she was upset. Nicole took the time to approach her to see if she was okay. She embraced her, included her and listened to her. When I met this young girl, she had grown through many of her difficult circumstances. She said because of Nicole's influence, she decided to begin ministering to other young girls who were struggling.

There were many stories I heard about how Nicole encouraged her competitors at the horse shows and helped the younger riders with their horses. Nicole had decided no matter how intense the competition was at any given horse show; her goal would be to make new friends at every single one.

Story after story brought us comfort and it was almost as if we were getting to spend a few more moments with Nicole with the hearing of each one. I do know it was difficult for some to share their Nicole stories with me. Frequently when someone loses a loved one, people feel awkward about talking to them about their loved one. They don't want to make the person feel worse or remind them of their pain. However, that is not the case with me or with many of the people I know. We want to hear our child or loved one's name. We want to hear how they impacted the world and their lives here mattered. We want to know they are not or will not be forgotten. We want to hear about their lives here and their interactions with others. I still on occasion will hear a story about Nicole I had never heard before. I still crave those stories and am delighted when someone shares with me a special memory they had with Nicole.

As the stories thinned out and became less frequent, it caused me to be sad and I tried to find a way to fill that need. That is when I read and re-read the cards and letters that had been sent to me. I believe when some of those cards were written, God was guiding the very hand that was writing them. He knew what day I would need to read a certain note, passage or encouragement. The simple gesture of taking the time to write down words of love gave me the courage to continue walking through every day.

So, if you know someone who has lost someone close to them, say their loved one's name. Tell them you are thinking of them or if you recall a particular memory that might bring them joy or make them smile. I have a few friends that still contact me every year on Nicole's birthday and her Heaven day. I usually don't answer the phone, and they never require a response from me, but I take so much comfort in those messages. Just to know Nicole isn't forgotten. I desire to be that kind of friend to others.

I do want to encourage some of you who may have the tendency to isolate in your pain to be careful not to go too far into your isolation. You may not feel like seeing or speaking to anyone and that is a normal response to what you've been through. However, while guarding your heart, let some trusted individuals in to your circle. You will need them, if not today, eventually. Let them help you, because helping you, helps them. Handling those relationships well was good for my healing and created lasting sources of support. Those people are still here for me nineteen years later, as I am for them.

I will also say it is important to protect your heart. Proverbs 4:23 tells us about the wisdom in guarding your heart. Sadly, there may be people who want to boss you around in your grief, making it their responsibility to tell you how you should feel. Don't allow anyone to hijack your sorrow and make it all about them. I found it helpful to have some "safe" friends near me that would run interference when that happened. It didn't happen often, but it is something of which to be aware.

I hadn't had many brave moments in my life prior to this, but the friends and family who were brave enough to come face-to-face with our sorrow and not look away, but love us through it, they gave me strength to take another step. Those stories of how Nicole was brave enough to approach people who were not like her and put herself out there to encourage others, gives me the courage today to try to look past the hard exteriors of some and love without condition. Courage is contagious.

- *Grief Note.* Guard your heart, but do not live in isolation. Allow trusted friends to reach you, to speak comfort, to be there. And don't be afraid to tell them what you need, then let them meet those needs.
- *Grief Note.* Look for the little gifts from God. It might be a letter, a phone call or an encounter with a stranger. God will bless you in the perfect timing and way, just keep your heart and eyes attuned to look for them.
- *Love Them Well.* Say their loved one's name. Share the stories. You won't hurt them by "reminding" them of their loved one...they've never forgotten. They've never not missed them. They think of their loved one often. It's nice to hear about or talk about their loved one. It's nice to not feel alone in thinking of them fondly.

Chapter 7:

The New Normal

"But He said to me, 'My grace is sufficient for you, for
my power is made perfect in weakness'"
(2 Corinthians 12:9a).

The long, wintery days were a time of great adjustment for our family. Because we are self-employed, Larry had to go back to work to keep things going. It was hard for him to leave me and the kids, but the business relied on his supervision. Before Nicole passed away, I worked in the office for the business. Afterward I was not able to go back to work in the same capacity for quite some time.

I had a very difficult time concentrating and even the slightest problem would cause me extreme anxiety. Our office manager Carole was such a blessing during that time. She had become a dear friend and part of the family, so after Nicole's accident, she stepped in and not only took over my responsibilities in the business, but also my personal bills and business. It took a long time to fully focus and concentrate again.

The Lord knew we would need someone special during that time and He sent Carole beforehand in preparation. With her taking care of the business side of things, I was freed up to turn the very limited focus I had toward the kids and getting back into some sort of schedule.

I'm very grateful I had the luxury of Carole's help when my focus was lacking. I know that isn't the case for everyone.

There were so many events and activities on our family calendar that suddenly had no purpose for us. They seemed to hang, suspended in a stinging limbo. I didn't know what to do with them. Nicole had been working diligently to try to earn enough points and qualify for the Youth Quarter Horse World show. We had purchased her show horse Neon just eight months before she went to Heaven. Her every waking moment consisted of completing her school work, then racing down to the trainer's facility to train and ride.

We also had horses at home for whom she and Lisa rode and cared. Every time I looked out at the barn or thought about Neon at the trainer's barn, it made me keenly aware of the missing part of my heart. I wondered at times if it had all been a waste, but always came back to those days at horse shows and in the barn. Those moments were priceless and gave me the gift of memories no amount of money could ever buy. I learned as raw as my heart felt when I was with the horses, if I embraced the rawness and those memories, it also brought a sense of comfort to me. The sleep-deprived days at the horse shows, watching Nicole work toward something she loved passionately, was breathtaking. She fought through many obstacles and roadblocks to be a victor. She was a fierce competitor and yet had the wonderful ability to reach out and help her opponents. Being with the horses enabled the memories to flow to me in a fresh, healing way.

I don't know if it was my imagination, but the horses seemed to miss her. They would nicker when I approached them, as if asking about her. The horses were not our only animals who missed Nicole. Her dog Nala had been her constant companion and was lost without her. She would wander around the house looking for Nicole before curling up near my feet. I found great comfort in having her near me. Actually, I think we brought comfort to one another.

In addition to the horses, Nicole was extremely involved at our church. She was a girls' small group leader and a Leader-In-Training (LIT) for Awana, a responsibility she took very seriously. The LIT's were also training for Awana Olympics the next year. Her Awana team worked hard after her death to participate in the Olympics in Nicole's honor. They ran their hearts out and won the gold medal in her name. There was not a dry eye in the house as they finished a hard-fought competition.

Nicole thrived in her busy schedule. However, after she went to Heaven, the schedule that brought so much movement to our lives came to a screeching halt for us. On the other hand, the rest of the world continued, much as it had before. That seemed illogical to me. How could the world continue to go on without her presence? How could the animals that she cared for so diligently still be here, while she was not? How could the sun come up and go down as it always had? How could companies and schools be open for business as usual? How was I supposed to go to the grocery store, educate my kids or even take a shower? It didn't make sense to me. How could all these normal things seem so abnormal?

You hear a lot these days about the "new normal." That is what our family had to discover. What was our "new normal?" I wish I could say discovering it went smoothly all the time. I don't know how it would look to do it well all the time. But we muddled through, eventually coming to a place of new routine. Still, every day brought painful reminders we were missing a huge part of what used to be "us."

Like a body recovering from a catastrophic injury, the body of our family had to learn to walk, eat, sleep, breathe and exist without her. Nicole and Lisa shared a room. It was their own uniquely, expressively fun space. They shared secrets in that room, laughed in that room, dreamed about their futures and even fought in that room. When Nicole left this earth, Lisa was left to live there alone. It was a constant reminder to her she had lost her buddy that she'd had since she was two-years-old. Together we decided to live in their room as it was before was too much for Lisa to bear day after day. So, we cleaned up the room and put everything perfectly in its place as it had been on 12/28/98. We preserved the memory of the room and the fingerprints of a special place in time by taking pictures of it. We photographed every square inch of it and gave Lisa, Megan and Alex the opportunity to take items that would bring them comfort. After that, we proceeded to pack all the cherished belongings Nicole had gathered throughout her life into crates.

The room felt empty and void when Nicole's earthly possessions were removed. The bunk bed that had obviously been meant for two people no longer served its purpose. How many nights had Lisa peeked over the top bunk and shared secrets with her best friend until they fell asleep? Now the bottom bunk lay empty, a glaring reminder of the missing part in Lisa's life; in all our lives. So, we put the bunk beds into storage and bought Lisa a futon. We painted the room blue and decorated with a cheerful, beach theme. It was a painful process, but a necessary piece for Lisa's healing as she moved into her new normal.

I have spoken to several moms who had to tackle this heart-breaking task. Some people find it best to donate and give away as much as possible, as quickly as possible. I do believe that, for most people, if you are able, it is best to wait a year before making big decisions about what to give away. But I do acknowledge since we all grieve in different ways, we have to find our way through the process the best we can.

I know for me, I had difficulty parting with anything that had belonged to Nicole. I did give a few things away to those who loved her, to bring comfort to them, but I kept everything else for a while. Everything. Socks, papers, everything Nicole had ever touched or thought to save. I carefully packed up the items that represented her physical life into crates for safe keeping. I labeled each crate: clothes, awards, pictures & misc.

Once those crates were packed away and labeled, I found myself with another category of material items of which I needed to make decisions. This category was even more difficult than the first. It was the category of "Lost Dreams."

Part of the "Lost Dreams" category included mail I received in her name. Most of it was just junk mail from different businesses to whom she had given our address. She was forever trying to win a boat or a truck in the mall and would fill out an entry form. She was just sure she would be the next winner. When I would receive mail with her name on it, I couldn't throw it away. I couldn't bear the thought of anything with her name on it going in the trash. One day I received a manila envelope addressed to her from Pacific Quarter Horse Association. As I opened it, a bittersweet realization washed over me. I pulled out two certificates with her name embossed in the center. She had placed in the top ten in California with her show horse Neon. It meant she qualified to receive a jacket with her winning events stitched on the front. I remembered how she dreamed about earning enough points with her horse to be able to wear one of those jackets someday.

My sadness was palatable as I grieved those lost dreams. It felt like a waste as I held those certificates in my hand. I could almost hear the Lord whisper to me that it was never a waste. Each moment was a gift and not about the award, but about the treasured memories and moments along the way. I chose to go ahead and get the jacket. It is now a lovely reminder of Nicole's hard work and dedication. She was able to be a part of something special and excelled at doing it.

Another "Lost Dream" was her graduation. Nicole went to Heaven half way through her senior year of high school. She already had her senior pictures taken and was making plans for a grand graduation celebration. While her friends were preparing for their graduation and for what college they would attend, we were packing up the physical items that represented her life. When I looked at her senior pictures, especially the ones of her in a cap and gown that she would never wear for its intended use, my heart broke. I had to remind myself again with the Lord's help those days were not wasted. I also had to remind myself she was not missing anything because, as awesome as all these experiences are, they are nothing compared to Heaven.

Every day that we walked through helped us establish the "new normal" for our family. Lisa had a year and a half left of high school, before heading off to college. Megan's teachers were very accommodating in helping her get caught up in her school work. Alex was still not completely adjusted to American life after only being with us for a short time. Now he had to adjust to another major life change, being separated from his biggest advocate and big sister. Every day we missed Nicole, even as we learned how to live in our new dimension.

In addition to my difficulty in concentrating, I was surprised when I was hit with the unexpected physical effects of grief. The emotional wounds of grief that manifested in physical ways startled me. There was a constant pressure on my chest. It was as if I could literally feel my heart breaking. I had very limited energy, in part because I had difficulty sleeping, which left me exhausted all the time. Even when I did get a good night's rest, I struggled to get through the day without a nap. I tried to reason it away by telling myself that I was fine physically and I should be able to get out of bed and get some things done. At first, I was too hard on myself and realized I had to learn to give myself room to heal physically, as well as emotionally.

I liken it to a physical amputation. When we lose a child or someone close to us, it is like amputating part of our very being. If I were to lose a leg, I wouldn't expect to just hop out of bed and walk around as if nothing ever happened. I would have to learn to walk again, in a whole new way. I would need rest to allow my body to heal. I would have to adjust my lifestyle to accommodate my missing limb. In the same way, when Nicole died, part of me was cut off and missing. I needed to rest more and learn to walk again in the new normal of life without her.

It is important to recognize these symptoms so they can be dealt with in a healthy manner. This is not to say it is healthy to give into our pain and let it define us. There is a delicate balance between pushing too hard and not pushing at all. Just as the person with an amputation or serious injury goes to physical therapy to slowly adjust to their new life situation, grievers need to do the same.

Joseph Mercola, DO, and leading holistic physician notes, "Exercise may fight feelings of depression better than antidepressants while relieving feelings of anxiety, pain, insomnia, fatigue, brain fog, and more." Continuing, he writes "If you're currently grieving, you needn't get bogged down with the details… simply get moving; any activity that appeals to you is worth it – hiking, swimming, yoga, group classes, dancing, and bicycling."

I have found this to be true and have seen the evidence of it in my life. Not only did I subscribe to this the first few years after Nicole's death, but I still do today when I find myself feeling the pressure of grief or anxiety.

Personally, I found it helpful to take small walks throughout the day. This became much easier as the long, cold days of winter began to subside. The warmer days of spring helped me to be outside at longer intervals and brought small flickers of hope to my soul.

It was vital for me to push myself in small chunks because I had the tendency to give into my grief and fall into despair. Being outside in God's creation fed my soul and helped me to feel closer to Him. On particularly difficult days, I could be found in the garden for hours at a time. I just needed to have my hands in the dirt, connecting me to Him. My body would be aching from the physical exertion, while my soul was being mended by God.

- *Grief Note.* If you are in the first few days, weeks or even months of a traumatic loss in your life, give yourself grace and space to heal, physically and emotionally. Some days that might just be getting out of bed for a little while and eating some food. Don't be surprised if you don't have energy or even if you experience flu-like symptoms. Please consult your doctor if any of these symptoms become severe.

- *Grief Note.* If you are walking through a difficult time and are frustrated because you are unable to think clearly or maintain focused thoughts, give yourself grace. These symptoms are a normal part of the physical aspect of your grieving process. If you are unable to have someone step in and help, take difficult tasks in small chunks. Allow plenty of breaks. Also remember it is an important time to keep things simple and minimal in your scheduling.

- *Grief Note.* Digging in the dirt may not be healing to you but find what is. Get outside, go for a walk, sit on the beach and soak in God's goodness every day if you can.

- *Grief Note.* Take small steps. Be intentional about taking care of yourself physically as well as emotionally. Try to get plenty of sleep, eat a well-balanced diet and avoid unhealthy escapes like drugs and alcohol.

- *Love Them Well.* Encourage your friend or family member to make healthy choices and partner with them. If they are up for a walk, give them company. If they want to garden, go to the nursery and help them choose plants that will bring a measure of joy.

- *Love Them Well.* Accept what your griever needs in order to heal. Whether it's wearing an article of clothing of their loved one who has passed, or putting things away quickly, don't judge.

Chapter 8:

Letting Go

*"There are always two choices. Two paths to take. One
is easy. And its only reward is that it's easy."*
– Author Unknown.

With Nicole missing from our physical world, I had
the tendency to make a shrine out of anything that
was a physical representation of her existence with
us. I held on to every material item that she had owned or even
anything that had her name on it. My grief created an urge in me
to cling to anything tangible to try and keep her close. I know
this is a natural response to missing her, but I could feel myself
holding onto these things in an unhealthy way. I was trying to fill
the void, but it was never filled. Consequently, I clutched onto
everything that even remotely had any connection to Nicole, and
it weighed me down with extreme pressure. I needed to have the
courage to let some of that go, and I did learn, a little at a time.

Our world is in a constant state of decomposition and regeneration. The circle of life in this fallen world is that eventually every physical thing here will degrade to leave space for the new. I knew that was a natural part of life, but I just didn't want to let go of one more thing after Nicole went to Heaven. I felt like I could not handle one more change in my life. I wanted to hold onto things just as they were, to preserve what little I had left of her. Deep inside I worried she would be forgotten and it would be like she never walked on the earth. (I now know she is not forgotten by those who loved her and never will be. I have wonderful friends and family who have made sure of that. I just felt like it at the time.)

Unfortunately, some things were taken away from me before I felt ready to let go. When that happened, I was devastated and felt as if I lost part of her all over again. I had saved every recording I could find of her voice. I had a voicemail from her saved on my phone and sometimes would listen to it, just to feel close to her. One day after having dinner out with the family, I got the urge to listen to her voice. As we were walking out to the car, I called my voicemail, so I could listen to her message when I was greeted with an automated announcement that the phone company was updating their system. I was instantly alarmed and called again, sure I had dialed wrong. It was the same message, so I called the phone company. I was told that during their system updates, all the voicemails were lost. I frantically explained the situation to the woman on the other line, explaining that there had to be some way to retrieve Nicole's message. She completely sympathized with my situation, but sadly explained that there was no way to recover Nicole's voice. It was gone forever. My sadness consumed me as I drowned in regret. I berated myself for not recording or securing her sweet voice. I was so angry with myself, but I had no choice other than to let go.

The voicemail is just one example of things I've had to let go that are representations of Nicole's life here. Another was the Christmas lights she and her boyfriend hung the Christmas before she went to Heaven. I knew in my heart it was impractical to expect the lights to remain as Kevin and Nicole hung them forever, but I tried. I was sad when they deteriorated beyond repair and could no longer stay where her hands had placed them.

One of the most agonizing parts of Nicole that I felt was taken away from me happened while I was at a two-day Women of Faith conference with the ladies from our church. It had only been a couple of years since Nicole had gone to Heaven. I didn't want to go and it had taken a lot of convincing for me to agree. I felt if I left home, then something bad would happen. I wanted to stay home, even though I knew in my heart it would be good for me. I also was concerned my emotions would get the best of me in a crowd and I wouldn't be able to escape. Once I arrived with the ladies and began to settle down and relax, I received a phone call from Larry. He was very hesitant and struggled to give me the news that Nala, Nicole's sweet dog, had been run over and killed. I felt like the ground was shaking under me and I began to question him, saying that it wasn't possible. I wanted to go home, but he assured me there was nothing I could do and that I needed to stay there with the ladies. My friends surrounded me and loved on me through that weekend. It was an important part of my letting-go process.

I could not see I had developed an unhealthy pattern of clinging on to things too tightly in my attempt to control my ever-changing world. That also caused me to develop the false belief that if I left home on a trip, something bad would happen because I wasn't there to control it. I became very angry with God. I felt like I had trusted Him and had done everything He had asked. Was nothing safe in this world? Was the comfort I drew from Nicole's dog too much to ask from God? Was I being punished for something? Those questions caused me to wrestle with my faith and I hate to admit it, but it caused me to question the goodness of God.

I won't attempt to answer the question that scholars have debated through the ages of "How could a good God allow so much suffering in the world?" I believe there are a lot of answers to that question, many of which will never be answered on this side of Heaven. I do believe He did give me some answers that spoke to my specific situation. Through Nala's death and other times I was forced to let go of the tangible things that reminded me of Nicole, God showed me I was grasping on to things that ultimately were temporary and brought no lasting comfort. I was essentially making those items almost like idols that were taking the place of God in my life.

According to 2 Corinthians 4:18, "we fix our eyes not on what is seen, but on what is unseen, since what is seen is temporary, but what is unseen is eternal."

I don't necessarily believe God caused Nala to be run over and killed or Nicole's voicemail greeting to be erased. These unfortunate events are things that happen in a world full of brokenness and problems. But I do believe through those experiences, God revealed I was allowing the physical things of the world to be my source of comfort and strength, instead of Him. I was looking to the comforts instead of the Comforter. I was also trying to control what I was never designed to control. Control is an illusion anyway. We really don't have the ability to control much outside of our reaction to our circumstances.

There is nothing wrong with enjoying the parts of Nicole I still have on this earth, as long as I keep it in balance. Recently, her horse Coco died at the ripe old age of thirty-three. Coco played a large part in Nicole's life and I was blessed she lived so many years after Nicole went to be with Jesus. I was sad when Coco died but enjoyed reminiscing about all the fun we had at horse shows with Nicole riding her. However, this time, it didn't consume me.

After we packed a large portion of Nicole's belongings in crates, we put the crates in storage. Over the years, I've gone through most of the crates slowly, deciding what to keep, what to give away, and what to donate. There were some items that just needed to be thrown away. Time has helped bring clarity to these painful decisions.

I feel like on this side of the grief, those decisions have been less traumatic. I am glad I was not forced to make a permanent decision about her belongings right away. I have been able to absorb those decisions gradually. Now when I open a crate with Nicole's belongings inside, it brings up less sorrow and more happy memories.

There are many things I leave out and easily accessible that help me to feel close to Nicole. I have some of her sweatshirts that I wear on a regular basis and my sister made me a beautiful quilt out of some of her clothes. I keep Nicole's cedar chest, in which she had stored pictures, Bible studies, journals and awards, in my office. Larry and I gave her the cedar chest on her sixteenth birthday. Traditionally, a cedar chest (sometimes also called a hope chest) was to store things a young woman would need for her future, possibly to set up house. Now, it holds her most prized possessions and the keepsakes that I want to have close. When I'm missing her most, I open the cedar chest. As the familiar scent drifts up, it makes me smile. I can lift out the treasures held within and my mind instantly visits a place in time. I thumb through her Senior Yearbook, the one she never held. Instead, it was tenderly held by grieving classmates who wrote words of love. Under her picture is her senior quote, "There are always two roads to take. One is easy, and its only reward is that it's easy." That's my girl! There is also a note she wrote me on a paper towel. "To Mom, I love you very, very mucho. I miss you, do you miss me? Love, Nicole." I can practically hear the words coming directly from her. Those are treasures that I am now able to visit and remember. I still work to maintain the balance of holding these precious memories loosely and letting go of what I must.

I did find it helpful to make a positive impact with what I chose to let go. For instance, if it was her clothes, I really tried to picture some young girl who could not afford some of the fun clothes Nicole wore and her being able to enjoy them. Donating her clothes or giving things away to those who needed them was good for my heart. I would remember Nicole's generosity and know that she would want me to bless others if I was able. I'm not done going through those crates, but I have allowed myself the space to tackle them in small chunks of time. For some, this may be like taking a bandage off slowly, when they just need to rip it off and do it all at once. There is no specific timeline, but I would encourage anyone to embrace the process and allow it to bring some healing.

Some of the letting-go process included me having to let go a part of Nicole's future plans. We made the difficult decision to sell her show horse Neon. We had purchased him only about a year prior. He was her dream horse and she planned to qualify for the AQHYA World Show. The competition was tough, but she worked hard to be able to earn enough points to qualify for the show. We kept our other horses, but it was not financially possible to keep Neon. Plus, it was unfair not to allow him to live up to his potential. Even considering selling him felt like another part of Nicole was being ripped away from me as I thought about all the plans she had for him. Our trainer found a buyer for him and arranged the details. Unfortunately, the day I met the buyers to sign the papers was on Nicole's birthday. She would have been eighteen-years-old. Instead of celebrating her birthday, I was selling her future plans. It was a hard day. As I signed the papers to transfer Neon over to his new owners, I tried to picture those young girls riding him and enjoying him as much as Nicole did. Last I heard they still owned Neon and he was doing great with them. That also does my heart good.

I also had to learn to let go of the expectations I placed on other people. I see now that I put unfair expectations on Nicole's siblings and friends. I desperately wanted them to live free, happy lives and fulfill their dreams. The problem was, it wasn't necessarily their dreams I wanted fulfilled. They were my dreams I placed upon them. I wanted to save each one of them from pain and disappointment. But despite my best intentions, it wasn't possible to do that for them. Every time I tried to rescue and fix someone, I stunted them. It wasn't my place to control the outcomes and journey for their lives. That was God's job. It's hard to love 100% and still hold on loosely.

As I learned that particular lesson, God showed me something amazing. When I let go of all the dreams I had for Nicole's siblings and friends, I was able to see the dreams God had placed in my heart. He had plans and a purpose for me, but as long as I focused on what I thought everyone else should be doing, I was too distracted to see it.

There are so many areas the Lord has worked in my life in letting go. Unfortunately, for much of it He had to pry my hands open, forcing me to let go. It hasn't only been the tangible, material things, Nicole's future plans or even the expectations I've had to let go. I've had to learn to let go and forgive.

Most of the forgiveness I've withheld is toward myself. I had to forgive myself for encouraging Nicole to be assertive and take her turn in riding the ATV that took her life. I had to learn to forgive myself for sometimes not being as patient as I should have been. I had to let go of all the times I chose work over spending time with her and not being attentive. I hate to admit it, but I had to forgive God. God didn't do anything wrong or doesn't owe me an explanation, but I was often angry at Him because of Nicole's death and the fact that He didn't prevent it.

Once I was able to let go of all the unforgiveness to which I was clinging, I realized how truly freeing the choice of forgiveness is. In some areas, I've had to do it over and over until I didn't have the urge to hold onto it any longer. Forgiveness doesn't condone the bad behavior, it just releases the responsibility of handling that to God. Bitterness is a heavy load to carry around on our shoulders.

- *Grief Note.* If you are currently drowning in the decisions on what to do with your loved one's earthly possessions, I give you permission to take your time. Don't allow the expectations of others to push you into making decisions you are not ready to make. On the contrary, if you feel the need to create new space for your new normal by packing away, donating or even discarding items that are weighing you down, I encourage you to do so. Do not allow the opinions of others to make you feel guilty, whether for keeping or discarding. If you do choose to discard items, you might offer them to friends or family members who may draw comfort from the items.

- *Grief Note.* If you are holding on to the stuff of this world, expectations, or unforgiveness and feel burdened under the weight of it all, I encourage you to open your hands and let it all go. God gives courage once we open our hands and give everything to Him. We are not meant to carry it all and He is so much more capable than we are.

- *Love Them Well.* Grief comes in waves. As time goes on, the waves spread further apart and are usually seen coming. However, when a giant wave crashes unexpectedly on your friend or family member, be patient and supportive. Sometimes the unexpected waves after significant time has passed are brutal. Love them through it and keep in mind grief is a journey, not something to "get over."

Chapter 9:

Protecting My Mind

*"Above all else, guard your heart, for everything you
do flows from it"*
(Proverbs 4:23).

E ven though my heart had the desire to live courageously
and victoriously, there was a fierce battle going on in my
mind. In some ways, the physical manifestations of grief
were easier to handle, because the effects were on the outside.
My emotions were extremely raw and on the surface. I was prone
to emotional meltdowns and quick to snap at people around me.
Even the slightest pressure could put me over the edge. Sometimes
I didn't even need a trigger. I was hyper-sensitive to everything.

I had thoughts of regret, wishing I could have re-do's on time
I neglected to spend with the kids. For instance, I never got to see
Nicole snowboard. The snow was powdery and the conditions
were perfect the winter before Nicole went to Heaven. Larry was

working close to home, so he was able to take the kids up to the local mountains often to learn to snowboard. Nicole caught on quickly and wanted me to see her new-found snowboarding skills. Unfortunately, our business was going through an IRS audit at the same time. I knew we had done things honestly, but I was very stressed out. I didn't want to miss anything when I saw the auditor. I spent long hours going through every income and expense with a fine-tooth comb. When Larry and the kids tried to get me to take a break and ride up to the mountains with them, I put them off with the excuse that I had to get ready for the audit. I let the anxiety of the audit distract me from what was more important. Because of that, there was never another chance to have Nicole show me how she had learned to snowboard.

Those types of regrets led to discouragement. I felt like I was in a constant battle for my mind, and in fact I was in a battle. Prior to Nicole going to Heaven, I knew I had to be careful with what I allowed in my mind, but in my grief, I had to become extra vigilant. When I read 2 Corinthians 10:3–5 I found there really was a battle for my mind. Verse 5 talks about learning to take my thoughts captive and making them obedient to Christ. When a destructive thought started coming into my mind, I had to capture it and decide: Is this true and positive or will this thought take me to a place of despair? I had to be diligent to keep my mind from despair because despair would lead me to a place of hopelessness. The opposite of despair is hope.

The Bible reminds me, "We do not want you to be uninformed about those who sleep in death, so that you do not grieve like the rest of mankind who have no hope" (1 Thessalonians 4:13).

This verse doesn't say not to grieve, but it does say that while grieving those who have gone on to Heaven before us, we can have hope. That hope is not some pie in the sky, false sense of wishing. The hope that we have as believers in Christ is real, solid and factual. So, I had to continually remind myself that Nicole was living, not only living, but more alive than anyone else left on earth.

I am a very visual person. Since I couldn't see Nicole, I would inevitably sink back into thoughts that Nicole was "gone." I had thoughts of her body in the ground and thoughts that I would never see her again. Those thoughts were not true. But because I couldn't see her, it is what I felt. Feelings are fickle, not always trustworthy or accurate. When that would happen, I would need to remember what 2 Corinthians told me. I was to literally capture that thought. I would have to ask myself if it was true according to scripture, not according to my emotions. If it was not true, then I was to make those thoughts obedient to Christ.

That seems easy to say on paper, but when my mind was being bombarded with images of Nicole's death, it was hard to fight that in my own power. Philippians 4:13 tells me I can do all things through Jesus, because Jesus gives me strength. I had no strength, but in my complete and utter weakness, God gave me strength. I was not always willing to do that. Sometimes, I just wanted to wallow in my pain, like a penance I needed to pay. However, God did not require any penance on my part. He just wanted me to take His hand. He would not force me to grieve with hope and to take my thoughts captive. But, with just the slightest yielding to Him on my part, I found that He came in and gave me the strength to battle the hopeless thoughts that were not from Him.

I found it difficult to just remove thoughts of hopelessness and leave an empty spot in its place. When I thought of Nicole's physical death and body in the ground, I found it helpful to replace to those thoughts with thoughts of her in Heaven. I know our minds aren't capable of fully grasping the wonder of Heaven, but I did feel like God would allow my imagination to have small glimpses of what it could be like. I could imagine her worshiping Jesus alive and free, not bound by time or the constrictions of this world. I would devour any book that was about Heaven and think about her in that setting. I'm thankful that God created us with an imagination, which, when conformed to the truth of the Bible, can bring hope.

"Finally, brothers and sisters, whatever is true, whatever is noble, whatever is right, whatever is pure, whatever is lovely, whatever is admirable…if anything is excellent or praiseworthy— think about such things" (Philippians 4:8).

This verse was a good reminder to me that it wasn't enough for me to capture the negative, despairing thoughts and getting rid of them. It was important for me to fill my mind with hopeful thoughts. Thoughts that were true. I could always find truth in the Bible, and so it was imperative that I kept scriptures close to me. Since I had a hard time concentrating, I couldn't memorize scripture as well as I wanted. Instead, I started writing verses on index cards and kept them easily accessible. I would also have sticky notes with verses and encouragement all over the place, so it would be directly in my line of sight often.

Sometimes I would struggle with thoughts of placing blame on myself or others for Nicole's death. If we hadn't gone on that trip or if the paramedics had done something different, she might still be here with me. One of the most destructive thoughts that I struggled with was that Nicole's accident was punishment for me because of past mistakes I had made, especially during my young rebellious years.

I was ashamed of the destructive decisions I made during my teens and early twenties. Shame can grip us and make us think things that are not true. Shame is not from God. He does not operate that way. He doesn't punish us by taking away someone we love. He forgives and restores us in all our ugly, messy choices.

The thoughts would come when I least expected it. It would hit me like a tsunami and threaten to drag me away from hope and into despair. Again, I would have to capture those thoughts and weigh them against scripture to determine if they were true.

Verses like Psalm 139:16 were really helpful to me during that time. It says all my days were written in God's book before they came to be. If that was true, then Nicole's days were also written in God's book. No actions of mine, past or present, could change the number of her days. No matter what the paramedics or doctors did or didn't do would have changed the outcome of that day. My past sins, however destructive, didn't cause God to take Nicole to Heaven early. Even though it felt early to me, I had to remind myself that she had a specific number of days on this earth to live. We all do.

It was vitally important for me to go through the process of capturing hopeless thoughts quickly, so I could rid myself of them. If I allowed destructive thoughts to come in and settle in my mind, it would take longer to bring my mind to a healthy place. Because there was a constant battle raging, I had to be very intentional about what I allowed to enter my mind. I had to not only be diligent to capture destructive thoughts, I had to be careful about what I watched on TV or at the movies. It is important for all of us, in any season of life, but particularly during a season when our minds are raw because of sorrow. If I watched a show portraying someone receiving CPR or being taken to the hospital in an ambulance, it would take me right back to December 28th. When that happened, I was opening myself up to feelings of hopelessness. My eyes were opened to how easily my mind is influenced by what I see. Even now, I try to be mindful about what I am viewing, asking myself if it is beneficial or is it something I should avoid. When I'm not careful, I can feel my thoughts slipping into areas they shouldn't.

Music can have a powerful influence on our thought life. Before Nicole went to Heaven, I played music constantly. However, after she passed away, especially at first, I had a hard time listening to music. Music can speak directly to the soul and can conjure up powerful emotions. After Nicole went to Heaven, my soul was so raw and fragile, it could not hold up under the weight of any added emotion.

Thankfully, over time, I have been able to enjoy listening to music again. Music still moves me emotionally, but now, with the Lord's help, I can channel those emotions in a way that brings hopeful thoughts. During the worship service at our church, I was able to imagine Nicole worshipping God along with me. It was as if the choir of Heaven and the congregation of our church were united in a moment that defied time and space. As the years have passed and I've lost others close to me, especially my parents, I will also imagine them worshipping before the throne of the Lord, me worshipping along with them. I can especially hear my dad's distinct voice when I do this.

Because music is such a powerful motivator, I have found it extremely helpful in the process of capturing my thoughts and making them obedient to Christ. There have been times I felt like I was fighting a losing battle, as discouraging thoughts bombarded me from every direction. Then, I felt God prompting me to put on some positive, good music and within moments, I could feel my heart steady and my thoughts begin to clear. Sometimes it is praise music, but sometimes it is rowdy, upbeat music like a battle cry for courage and strength. It's a good thing that I am usually alone when this happens, because I think the Lord is the only One who can appreciate my singing and dancing. When I am down or need to re-center my thoughts, I can just begin to sing and feel the depression being pushed back.

There are countless examples in the Bible of the power of music. The prison chains were loosened and gates were opened, as a result of Paul and Silas's singing praise to God (Acts 16). The enemy of Judah was pushed back and defeated when the Israelites sang of the enduring love of God in 2 Chronicles 20. Even the Psalmist reminds us to "Shout for joy to the Lord, all the earth Worship the Lord with gladness; Come before Him with joyful songs" (Psalm 100:1–2).

In the deepest pain of my grief, I found courage and strength in singing and speaking God's truth in gratitude to Him. Because I believe there is power in the spoken word, I believe words matter. Especially when I am fighting the battle of my mind, I try to filter the words I hear through music, radio or conversations. According to Proverbs 18:21, the words I speak have the power of life and death! I ask myself if the words I am exposed to or that I am exposing others to is beneficial or damaging. Not that I have this perfected, but when I am intentional with words, my mind is guarded and protected.

Even with all of this, there are times the voices of regret, defeat and discouragement scream louder than all the rest. Sometimes the only way to shut out all the negative voices is to get away and have some solitude time with the Lord. My friend Kat has encouraged me to schedule some deliberate and designated time alone with God. Her advice is to turn off everything. Social media, the phone calls, texts and even music has to be shut down, so I can listen clearly to God. If I can spend the time with the Lord enjoying His creation, even better. My senses are far more in tune to Him when I am in nature. There have been times I've been tempted to use this time to get caught up on some motivational reading, but even that takes my attention away from hearing the voice of God. It is hard at first because my brain is going a million directions and so accustomed to all the notifications and constant access to everything. Sometimes it helps me to focus on one verse or even one word, asking the Lord's direction. The important thing is that it is intentional and uninterrupted.

In the early days of grief, I didn't always recognize the importance of protecting my mind as hopeless thoughts ran rampant. Gradually the Lord showed me the importance of protecting my mind and diligently guarding my thought life. The seed of all we are and all we do is planted in the soil of our minds. That is where living victoriously is decided.

The definition of victorious is: to be the winner in a contest or struggle, defeating an adversary. To defeat an adversary, you must face whatever is threatening to destroy you. We have a very real adversary that is attempting to devour and defeat us (1Peter 5:8) and the battle starts in our minds. The good news is the Lord equips us with the weapons we need to have courage in the battle. He has destined us to be victors, not victims in the battlefield of our minds.

- *Grief Note.* Remember that God is a Loving Father, not a vengeful dictator. Death is the result of a fallen world. This is not a punishment for previous choices. God knew the number of our loved one's days before one came to pass.
- *Grief Note.* Use the gifts God has given. If music speaks to your soul, allow it to aid in your healing. If artwork speaks to you, find a museum. If nature brings

you comfort, set aside time to enjoy God's creation. Be intentional.

- *Grief Note.* Schedule alone-time with God, free from distraction and disruption. Allow the Healer and Comforter to touch your heart and mind.
- *Love Them Well.* Remind your friend or family member of God's unending kindness. Remind them what they believe when they begin to doubt.
- *Love Them Well.* The tongue holds the power of life and death. Before you speak (or text or email,) consider if your words are edifying and encouraging or bring harm or pain to your loved one. You may not agree with them on everything, including how they are grieving. But do not add to their burden of pain with unsavory words. Speak life. Speak love.

Chapter 10:

Laughter and Joy

"A cheerful heart is good medicine, But a broken spirit saps a person's strength"
(Proverbs 17:22).

In the midst of the winter of my grief, I had all but given up the idea I would ever experience the light-hearted season of spring. Spring represented color, life and joy. I felt like I was destined to walk in the cold, colorless winter of my sorrow. Eventually the cold, dark days of winter subsided and spring arrived. However, the hope of spring had not managed to seep into my heart. I had learned to walk through the daily routine of life, but it was just that—routine. I found myself in a flat, colorless place of existence. Joy seemed to elude me as I walked through my days.

I wondered if I would ever be able to laugh again. I mean really laugh, deep from my body until my stomach ached. Our family used to experience that type of laughter, but it was different after Nicole went to Heaven. It was a challenge to think of us laughing like that again.

I remember one time specifically, while Nicole was still with us, of trying to be productive and get something done around the house. I can't remember exactly what task we were trying to complete. It actually seems so unimportant now. The kids were goofing around and I became exasperated with their silly antics. Exhausted, I laid down on the couch. I was talking to the girls about the importance of accomplishing whatever it was we were trying to get done. Instead of taking me seriously, much to my dismay, Nicole took the comical a step further. She came and laid right on top of me and just laid there laughing. She refused to get off. I tried to be stern as I told her to get off and get her stuff done. Every word I said only made her laugh harder. Then, against my will, I started laughing. I began to poke her in the sides in an effort to get her up, but it didn't work. It only made her squeal each time I poked her and we both laughed even harder. The other kids joined in the madness and we all fell into a heap of hilarious chaos. We laughed until we cried and our sides throbbed in wondrous pain. I don't know if we ever got done what I was trying to accomplish, but I do know it was worth it if we didn't.

Nicole brought a delightful, lightheartedness to our lives. Being near her was like living perpetually in the color and joy of spring. It wasn't that she was foolish or unwise. As a matter of fact, she was extremely thoughtful and contemplative. She was intentional in what she chose to put her efforts. She persevered through any obstacle to achieve her goals. Even still, she brought color to the mundane, ushering the commonplace into the joy of the moment. She truly did live up to the meaning of her name, "Victorious Heart." She was brave enough to go outside of perimeters of the routine and see the wonder of the moment.

After she went to Heaven, everything felt gray. It seemed impossible to imagine experiencing color again. It was like the color and laughter of our world left when Nicole did. I wanted to be brave like her. I wanted to have a Victorious Heart and be full of joy. However, even if I could begin to imagine it, finding the humor in life didn't feel right. I thought if I laughed, I diminished the significance of losing of her. To be brave enough to laugh again and still honor losing her felt like a contradiction. I carried the belief if I laughed or even found joy in something, I was somehow forgetting about her.

Eventually I saw how futile and false this thinking was. I wasn't lessening Nicole's memory by laughing. I was actually honoring her by enjoying the moments God gave me here. If I was going to have a Victorious Heart like she did, I needed to be brave enough to allow joy back into my life. It took courage because in some ways it was easier to remain in the gray, colorless life. There was pain there, but it was a constant pain, one to which I had become accustomed. Once I chose to allow joy in, I knew there would be risk of a sharper kind of pain as the color shot in through my gray, predictable existence.

The thing about joy is that it is often coupled by sorrow. If I was going to allow myself to feel, then I couldn't pick and choose what I would feel. Gray was dull and unfeeling, but color was wild and unpredictable.

I realized this one day as I was driving in the car alone some months after Nicole went to Heaven. I can't remember the exact memory that came to mind, but it was something about Nicole that brought a smile to my face. It may have been a memory of the girls breaking out into a Veggie Tales song about why everyone needs a water buffalo. I think they knew every word to all the Veggie Tales songs, complete with acting it out. I remember being surprised that I smiled at the memory. A little color shot into the gray of my day. I savored the moment. But just as suddenly, the color brought with it a wave of grief. Grief over what was lost, those sweet moments never to be repeated, and I began to sob uncontrollably. The pain was unbearable and I felt like I was losing any ground that I had gained in the grieving process. There seemed to flow from deep inside me a sorrow that could not be quenched. I hadn't even been aware it was there. My body couldn't contain the pain and, in the solitude and safety of my car, I screamed out, as long and as loud as I could. I screamed over and over until I couldn't scream any longer. I could not handle the pain. It was too risky to feel joy or even recall a sweet memory, because to do so required a possible opening for pain.

Before Nicole went to Heaven, I thought God would not allow anything to happen to one of my kids because I could not handle the pain and oppressive grief. That was not right, thinking God wouldn't give me more than I could handle. This was far more than I could handle. Instead, God promises to carry me through anything. **He** would handle it. **He** would keep me from going into despair. I just had to be brave enough to hand Him the pain. This would be required of me if I were to have a Victorious Heart. I really did have a choice, I could live my days out in the gray and survive this pain. But the Bible says in Romans 8:37 that God is for us and "In all these things, we are more than conquerors through Him who loved us." That sounds like a Victorious Heart to me. My choice—gray or color; defeated or Victorious. I knew enough to know that I could not accomplish this on my own power. But after the flood of emotions poured out of me, God was offering me His hand. He was offering to pick me up and carry me through my pain. Part of Him carrying me through it meant that He would bring joy back into my life.

My spirit was broken because of grief. I would never "get over" losing Nicole or finish grieving the loss of Nicole like some task on a to-do list. I did, however, have the choice of allowing grief to define me and stealing the possibility of experiencing joy once more. To laugh was to experience life fully and bring mending to my broken heart. Research shows that laughter truly is good medicine. It not only feels great to our hearts, but it releases stress and boosts our immune systems. Laughter is actually good for our health and is the balm that brings healing to our broken hearts.

I longed to allow the healing of laugher into my life. I didn't want to reside in the broken, colorless place I was in, empty of joy. I wanted to honor Nicole's life and the life the Lord gave me by experiencing a cheerful heart. I did want to laugh again until my belly hurt and get carried away singing Veggie Tales. So, I chose in that moment to have courage and allow the possibility of laughter to filter in.

At first, I would avoid anything that had the possibility of bringing up emotion. I would try to steer clear of people, places, songs, even scents that would stir up too much feeling. This was part of my lifelong habit of seeking out safety and comfort. I avoided the uncomfortable and painful so I would be safe. The problem with being safe, is it is just that. Safe, but no growth and stagnant. As long as I avoided the painful places, I was stuck, unable to move through it. A friend who was widowed at a young age used a quote at her husband's memorial service that had become a powerful anthem for them in their journey of his terminal illness. "A ship in the harbor is safe, but that's not what ships are built for" (John Shedd).

So, I had to choose to allow areas of vulnerability in my life. Part of this thinking was beneficial for me because I discovered my grief came in spurts. Years ago, when I got my hair highlighted, the hairdresser would put a foam cap on my head and use a pulling device to reach through the holes in the cap to pull small strands of my hair through. I've likened my grief to that highlighting process. It hurt sometimes when she pulled my hair through the small holes, but it was just a little at a time. God knew my mind could not take the full load of my grief all at once. Some people told me I was in shock, some told me it was denial. But I believe God allowed me to be in the gray a while for my protection. It may not be like this for everyone, but for me, once I decided to allow color in, it was a little at a time. So instead of avoiding all the places and situations that would stir up my grief, I would risk one or two at a time. This was more manageable for my heart and I was able to embrace the joy as well as the pain.

It didn't happen overnight, but joy and laughter did come back into my life. I don't think it is as frequent as it was back when Nicole was with us. Those of us who have lost a part of our hearts realize there is a fragile side to our life and we are changed. Grief doesn't have to define us, but it does become a fundamental component of who we are. It is always a part of us and that is not necessarily a bad thing.

Sorrow helped me to see with more clarity the important things of life. As the sharpness of my pain decreased, my desire to honor Nicole's memory by living well increased. Part of living well meant seeking out ways in which to usher joy back into my life.

The most significant thing that helped me in the process was to let go of the guilt I had because I thought I was leaving Nicole behind by incorporating joy and laughter back into my life. My emotions told me I was not honoring her if I smiled or laughed. But those feelings were pure lies. I reminded myself to follow her example and be brave enough to live my life well. This was the best way I could honor Nicole. Even more than that, it honored God's gift of my own life, to be present and make every moment count. I would even try to picture what Nicole would say to me if she were here. She would tell me not to take myself too seriously, to work hard, be intentional, love people and laugh a lot.

It took practice and it may seem strange to say it, but I would actually practice smiling. It felt silly at first, smiling for no reason, but I would practice walking into a hard situation with a smile on my face. Little by little, my emotions would catch up to my smile. In the same way, I also practiced laughing. If I heard a joke that I knew was funny, but didn't really feel the humor in it, I would purposefully laugh. It seemed fake, but it really worked. It was like using muscles I had not used in some time. I needed to get them back in shape so they would perform correctly.

From what I've observed, there can be an opposite effect as well. If we choose to completely submerse ourselves in the pain, allowing our grief to define us, then the healing process can be stunted. We can be so saturated in the loss of our loved one that we become bitter, angry and hardened. This can lead to an isolating life, convincing ourselves that no one understands our pain. If we allow ourselves to stay in that place, it can cause us to disconnect with family members and friends, even to the point of being angry they are finding joy in their lives. In everything, balance is the healthiest course.

I still have to fight the gray when I get caught up in worry or anxiety. I have to remember the joy of the Lord is my strength and He has me covered. When I feel the gray washing over me, I have to remind myself of the simple times and how I shouldn't have sweat the stuff that I couldn't change. Now, it has been many years since Nicole has been gone and I still sometimes find myself surprised when I laugh until I can't breathe; I love the feeling that brings to my soul. The other night Larry and I were talking with my sister and her husband. The conversation started toward the humorous and we all started laughing. Laughter is contagious, so we all were carried away in the hilarity of the moment. I thought of Nicole and wondered if she were laughing from Heaven with us and possibly poking me in the sides this time.

- *Grief Note.* Laughter and joy are not betrayals of your loved one. Rather, finding joy again is a way to honor their life and the joy they brought.

- *Grief Note.* While God has given you life and breath, He still has purpose for you. Allow His purpose-filled life for you to include joy. And remember, "The joy of the Lord is your strength" (Neh 8:10). It is not only okay, but good and helpful, hopeful and healing to embrace the joy of the Lord.

- *Love Them Well.* As your friend is learning to find joy and laughter again, share in their joy. Don't be afraid to laugh with them, even belly laugh! While it is good to be sensitive and follow their lead, you do not need to feel like you are on eggshells or must always be somber in their presence.

Chapter 11:

Unanswered Questions

"As the heavens are higher than the earth, so are my ways higher than your ways and my thoughts than your thoughts"
(Isaiah 55:9).

It is the natural inclination of a parent to want to protect their children, so after the shock of losing Nicole began to wear off, the questions began to flood my mind; the big one being, "Why?" Why was I not able to protect her? Why would God allow her to be taken when He knew what it had the potential to do to me?

I think in today's culture, we feel as if we have a "right" to have all the answers. If we are curious about something, we can just do a search on the internet and find the answer almost instantly. We feel "entitled" to have the answers to all the mysteries of life.

I believed God must have a huge purpose for taking Nicole to Heaven. I reasoned if I could find the answers to all my questions, especially the question of why, then I would be able to make some sense of it. After all, didn't Roman 8:28 say that God would work everything for the good of those who love Him? I loved God, so I knew He was working everything to the good in my life. But I wasn't prepared for the truth that God wasn't obligated to give me the answers to all my questions. Every time something good would happen as a result of Nicole's death, I would point to it and say, "There it is, there is the reason why." Each time I would walk away thankful for those blessings. But then my grief would remain, and it never felt like I could grasp the grand purpose of it all. I realized the question of why God does anything is too large for my spirit to contain.

There have been more questions than just why. Why wasn't I able to protect her? What if I had done something differently? Why didn't I pay attention more when Larry spoke of his concerns of losing a child? And most painfully, was I being punished for choices I had made in the past? Most of the questions have been left unanswered. God is not required to answer to me. The questions caused me to doubt my faith sometimes, but ultimately strengthened my relationship with God. I have not received the answers to my questions, but my view of God expanded.

When Job of the Bible went through unprecedented trials one right after another, his friends went on a tirade in an attempt to explain to Job all the reasons he had suffered much sorrow. Their quest to answer the question of why only brought more pain to Job's already broken heart. I have not experienced trials to the extent of Job, but after questioning God, I do understand what he meant when he said, "I had only heard about you before, but now I have seen you with my own eyes" (Job 42:5).

God does not hold it against us when ask questions of Him. According to Romans 8:26a, "the Spirit helps us in our weakness." Just a few verses later, God's Word says, "What, then, shall we say in response to these things? If God is for us, who can be against us? He who did not spare His own Son, but gave Him up for us all—how will he not also, along with Him, graciously give us all things? ...No, in all these things (sufferings) we are more than conquerors through him who loved us" (Romans 8:31–32, 37).

When Nicole died, I felt like anything but a conqueror. Because her name means Victorious Heart, I was drawn to words like Victorious, Brave, Courage and Conqueror. I wanted those words to describe me. But I could never conjure those attributes up on my own. Maybe that is why I asked all the questions. If I could get all my questions answered, I could be all of those things. But I am weak. I felt lost and crushed in my sorrow. Powerless on my own, but with the slightest yielding of my will to God, He began to make me more than a conqueror. In my weakness, He infused me with His strength, (2 Corinthians 12:9). The question I needed to ask myself was not the question of why, but the questions, "Would I trust the Lord with my unanswered questions and pain? Was I willing to trust in His goodness when the situation didn't feel good?" I professed to believe in God's goodness before Nicole died, but would my prior convictions hold up under the weight of my pain?

"As the heavens are higher than the earth, so are my ways higher than your ways and my thoughts than your thoughts" (Isaiah 55:9).

There is a reason I could not answer all the questions— because I am not God. I was only seeing Nicole's death from my small corner of eternity. God's ways are multi-faceted, and He is omnipresent. I will never be able to answer the reason of why on this side of Heaven and may not even on the other side.

I think in some ways my desire to answer all the questions was born from the desire to control. If I could figure out all the answers, then I could somehow control bad things from happening. Logically, I know there are very few circumstances I can control in this life. But emotionally, it doesn't always compute. In all my years as a mama, I knew generally where my kids were and what they were doing. Since Nicole was the oldest, I hadn't even experienced the launching of my kids into adult life as they left our home. For the first time as a parent, I couldn't reach one of my children. It was a feeling of near panic, because I was accustomed to being able to reach Nicole if I needed to. This was before everyone had a cell phone, but she had a pager and I could send a page for her to call me or leave a message at her friend's house. We were connected and our lives were intertwined. Suddenly, she was beyond my reach and I struggled to make sense of it.

Through much wrestling, I see now when I finally did relinquish the control of having to know why to God, my heart was able to experience His peace and comfort. It is His place to know why and for His purposes alone. In His purposes, there are many blessings I've seen as a result of Nicole's influence. Because she left us so suddenly and so soon, it has created in me a desire to be intentionally present and live fully while I am here. Nicole had a mission statement written down that I found in her Bible. It said she wanted to change the world one person at a time. Her mission statement has birthed a desire in me to be more outwardly focused to the people around me.

There are countless other blessings, if I just watch for them. There were several people who became Christ-followers as a direct result of attending Nicole's memorial service. One stands out in my mind in a profound way. A young man who was well acquainted with church and God realized through a series of events at the memorial service that he wasn't right with God. He made the decision that day to completely surrender and follow the Lord and it changed his life. I saw him several years later with his wife and children. He is a great husband and dad, leading his family in the Lord. Because of what he witnessed at Nicole's service, the course of his life was altered and is affecting the future generations through his children. That is a big deal, but for God, it is just one small facet of what He is doing through Nicole's death. It not for me to analyze or figure it all out. It is just for me to be grateful that I can be a witness to an amazing work that God is doing.

There are beautiful children, some of whom are now young adults, who are named after Nicole and that makes my heart happy. God enabled relationships to be formed because of the special bonds created through Nicole. Lives are changed because Nicole touched others through the way she lived and by her example. Those are all sweet blessings. When I let go of trying to find the purpose in her death, it freed me up to see the blessings as gifts and be grateful.

I had the comfort of having a good relationship with Nicole and being on good terms with her when she left this earth. What about those precious mamas that don't? What about those that have died that we are not sure about their eternal destination? Are they in Heaven? These are cruel and difficult questions.

It may seem easy for me to say, but I do believe the same principle applies in those situations. We don't know what happens in a person's soul in the moments before they go to eternity. I know 2 Peter 3:9 says, "The Lord is not slow in keeping his promise, as some understand slowness. Instead he is patient with you, not wanting anyone to perish, but everyone to come to repentance." This verse gives me confidence the Holy Spirit is whispering to everyone's soul, working and desiring that they would yield to Him. I also encourage those who struggle with their loved one's eternal fate to recall the thief crucified next to Jesus Christ. In Luke 23:40–43, Jesus rewards a thief who acknowledges His holiness with eternal life. This thief was close to death with no opportunity to right the wrongs he committed in his life. Another encouraging passage for those with these very real questions is the parable of the vineyard workers found in Matthew 20:1–16. God is generous, loving and wants to welcome all His children, regardless of when they find Him. Finally, Romans 8:27 says that God, "searches our hearts and He knows the mind of the Spirit (the Holy Spirit), because the Spirit intercedes for God's people in accordance with the will of God." This shows us the Holy Spirit is not only constantly drawing us to God the Father, but He is also interceding and praying for us.

Not only does God give me assurance and strength in the midst of all my unanswered questions, I believe He is close to me when I am grieving. "The Lord is close to the brokenhearted and saves those who are crushed in spirit" (Psalms 34:18).

I know God is always with me, but I know He is even closer when I am crushed in spirit. I believe He was near and all around me on December 28, 1998. Preparing me, holding me and sustaining me. He was with me when I witnessed Nicole riding the ATV off the dune. He was there as I helplessly watched our truck drive away with Larry and Nicole in the back to meet the paramedics. He heard me as I earnestly begged Him to spare her earthly life.

He didn't turn away from me, His eyes were turned toward me, and I believe it grieved Him deeply as my heart broke. Not because her death made Him sad, but because He sees the big picture. He sees it all and life here is just a tiny fraction of the big picture. What we see here and are experiencing here is so temporal and what we don't see, He sees. Eternity. (2 Corinthians 4:18). I think He grieved with me because He loves me completely. He knew losing Nicole would cut me so deep that I thought the wound would never heal. He knew I would doubt His love and doubt Him, but He stayed close to me even still.

God weeps with us in our sorrows, like he did with Mary when her brother Lazarus died (John 11). Jesus was not weeping over Lazarus, He knew He would be raising him from the dead. But, more importantly Jesus knew Lazarus would be with Him in eternity, despite his final earthly death. I believe He had compassion for Mary's pain. Earthly death brings separation and separation causes sadness. Tears are a natural response to that sadness. But what I love is our tears are never wasted or ignored by the Lord. He is close to us in our brokenness and sees each one of our tears. "You keep track of all my sorrows. You have collected all my tears in your bottle. You have recorded each one in your book" (Psalm 56:8).

Imagine that, He keeps track of the sorrows of all His people. He collected my tears. He collects your tears as well. The tears you cry when your heart is crushed because you can't hold your baby. In my weeping when all I wanted to do was to see Nicole again. Every tear is precious to Him. The tears shed because all the dreams are shattered beyond repair and hope is unimaginable. They are recorded in His book. There are no wasted tears.

I don't know why bad things happen and parents have to bury their children. Even if I had all the answers, it wouldn't lessen my sorrow. My heart would still break. What does bring comfort is that God, the one who does have all the answers, is close to us in our sorrow. He takes all of it and works it for the good. For His glory, He makes a beautiful thing out of our broken hearts.

When we see God in Heaven, all of the questions we had on earth will fade in the light of eternity. We will experience true clarity for the first time.

- *Grief Note.* You will have unanswered questions. This is inevitable. Our minds cannot understand the greatness and fullness of an eternal God. However, God is okay with us, His children, asking. He is not offended. Choose to continue to trust Him in spite of and because of who He is.

- *Love Them Well.* When your friend or family member asks tough questions, pray with them. Listen. Do not patronize, nor give false answers or false hope. Go to the Word together. And be okay with unanswered questions.

Chapter 12:

Birthdays and Holidays

*"Rejoice with those who rejoice; mourn with those who
mourn"*
(Romans 12:15).

Losing Nicole added a new dimension to birthdays, anniversaries and holidays. I always looked forward to celebrating traditions for milestones and holidays. But after Nicole's passing, I started dreading the approaching dates. Those days only amplified the obvious void left in our lives without Nicole. It wasn't just me, the rest of the family could feel it as well. Maybe it was because they could see it in me.

Birthdays came and went that first year for our family. I know the first year I probably didn't handle each one in the best way possible. Over the years, I've learned to adjust to the kids' birthdays, learning to make it more about them and less about me missing Nicole. Celebrating life, while realizing the fragility of life. In many ways, birthdays took on a deeper meaning. Each one of the kids are different and had different reactions to life without Nicole. I tried, not always successfully, to look at what type of activities spoke to their hearts and go in that direction. However, sometimes we had to go in a completely different direction, especially for Lisa's birthday. Her birthday was only a week to the day after Nicole's birthday. They had a lot of the same circle of friends from school and church, so it normally worked out better to celebrate their birthdays together. Lisa almost had to re-establish her identity on her own, without her big sister and constant companion. We tried to adjust accordingly.

I had to try to fight having unrealistic expectations when it came to the kids' birthdays. I felt like each person's celebration had to be the best birthday ever. That was not always helpful or healthy. Grief will sometimes do that to us. It seems to amplify what is already inside of us. God had to teach me, and honestly is still teaching me, how to have a healthy balance in these areas. Simplicity and just spending time together is the most important thing. I have a tendency to try to pack in so much that things are rushed, not taking the time to savor the preciousness of the moment.

The month of May brings mixed emotions for me. I love spring as the chill of winter melts away, the days are longer and the sun seems to warm up my soul. However, the month of May also carries hard dates—Mother's Day and Nicole's and Lisa's birthdays. In more recent years, May 11 marks the day that my mom went to be with the Lord.

The first May after Nicole went to Heaven was the hardest and was filled with plenty of mixed emotions and questions. There would be times I would just long to skip over those hard days. But I knew in the deepest part of me, I really wouldn't. To celebrate the day of Nicole's birth is to celebrate a beautiful life and brought lots of joy into my world. It was good to acknowledge her birth and life. Even in my deepest pain, I would never want to erase each and every moment I got to spend with her. I found it healing and healthy to embrace her birthday.

The first year, we went to the cemetery and released eighteen purple balloons in honor of her 18th birthday. We have released purple balloons several times on her birthday since, but every year is different. I've had to adjust as our lives and family has changed, but even if it is just me, I try to be intentional about embracing that day with joy and gratitude.

My friend Wendy recently shared how she honors her son Brendan on his birthday and Heaven day:

My twelve-year-old son, Brendan left us for Heaven on 3/26/13 after a five-week battle with a terminal brain stem cancer called Diffuse Intrinsic Pontine Glioma (DIPG). As you can imagine, it was and has been the most devastating thing that has happened to our family.

When a child dies, there isn't a manual to tell you how to handle it. You are not only left in shock but worried that your child will be forgotten. This is and will always be my biggest fear.

Every day is difficult but when a special holiday comes up, it makes that day even more difficult when your child isn't there to celebrate it. Because of this, I've tried to honor my son in ways that help keep his memory alive as well as make his birthday and Heaven day extra special days to celebrate his life.

Some of the ways that our family chooses to celebrate Brendan's birthday is that we always release his favorite color (green) balloons in the quantity of the years that he would have been. This last year, Brendan would have turned seventeen years old and so we released seventeen green balloons with notes to him, telling him how truly special he is to us and how very much we miss him. We go out to eat at his favorite restaurants and have purchased his favorite toys to donate to a foundation that encourages children with cancer and their families. We also purchase a cake and sing happy birthday to him, candles and all. This is the way that we choose to celebrate his birthday and what helps to get us through the day.

When Brendan's Heaven day comes along, it's always a really difficult day. For the first three years on Brendan's Heaven day, we had a gathering at his site at the cemetery and released green balloons while we played some of his favorite worship music. We've also released white doves as well. As time has passed we have decided to honor Brendan's Heaven day in a quieter, more personal way. We go to his site at the cemetery as a family and we release green balloons and place flowers there for him. We also eat at some of his favorite restaurants. It's just what helps us get through such a tough day.

The one thing I've learned since Brendan left us for Heaven is that there is no one way you have to celebrate or honor your child. You can do one thing one year and then do something different the next year. Some years you may feel more up to doing something and other years, it's all you can do to get through the day. Whatever it is that you choose, I pray that you find comfort in it and that even though it's such a difficult

day to get through, God will give you a peace in your
heart for the way that you choose to honor your child.
You know your child better than anyone else and it's
okay. It's okay to do what you need to do.

Mother's Day can be challenging, especially since my own
mom went to be with the Lord so close to Mother's Day. The first
few Mother's Days after Nicole went to be with Jesus, Larry gave
me a Mother's Day card from Nicole. That was a special way for
him to acknowledge that even though she is not here, I am still
her mom.

Each holiday, each year bring unique changes and challenges
to my life as I've learned to constantly adjust without Nicole.
As life has continued, I've had to also make adjustments as my
mom and dad went to Heaven, then as the kids grew up and
moved away from home. That also brought changes. Each one of
those changes bring an element of grief, because in some way or
another, it can represent loss.

While everyone is gathered together to celebrate holidays
like Easter, Thanksgiving and Christmas, it can be a painful
reminder of those that are missing from the holiday festivities. I
remember having the urge to call my mom and ask her about her
Thanksgiving dinner recipes for years after she we gone.

I have a friend named Chris that calls and leaves me a
message every year on Nicole's birthday and on her Heaven Day.
I rarely answer the phone, but Chris does not take offense, she
just leaves me a message. She assures me that she loves me and
she is thinking about me and Nicole on that day. These messages
mean the world to me, so much so, that I have several years of
messages still saved on my voicemail.

Grief seems to scream louder during the holidays. The hurt
may be years old, but the dull ache in the heart lingers under the

surface. It also could be that the hurt is recent and fresh, like a ripping open of our very souls and we can't seem to find our footing. The thought of an empty chair at our holiday table seems to multiply the sorrow we live with daily.

Everyone has different seasons or months that may elevate the pain of loss. It may be an annual event that you and your child went to every year or a special tradition that you observed for Easter or Christmas. For me, May and December have been typically my most difficult months. The pain has eased over the years and is not so sharp, but even still I am aware of it as those months draw close.

Since Nicole went to be with Jesus on December 28th, Christmas is heavily affected by that. Many years have passed since then, but each year as the holiday season approaches, I feel that old familiar ache in my chest. The grief still pushes me to tears as I crack open the boxes of Christmas decorations and see the stocking with her name embroidered along the top. What I wouldn't give to see her empty the contents of that stocking and hear her sweet voice say, "Thank you, Mama."

The first Christmas without her was the hardest. The thought of putting up Christmas decorations as if nothing ever happened seemed absurd, so we decided to try to go away for the holidays. We were so blessed when a gracious family offered to loan us their house in the mountains for Christmas, so we could just get away together. It was a huge place with room enough for extended family and was a blessed time of healing, being a safe place for us all to express our grief. I wonder if that family has any idea what an amazing gift that was to us.

Even though I had no choice on the loss of my precious girl, I did come to learn that I had a choice on how I reacted to the loss. I had and still have a choice every day and every holiday on whether I will receive God's comfort in gratitude or dwell on my pain.

Just as with birthdays, it is important to be intentional about slowing down and creating pockets of time to reflect and rest during the holidays. Be careful not to isolate yourself, but don't feel like you need to say yes to every party or gathering.

Our culture has certain expectations of what the holidays should look like and what traditions should be honored religiously. For me, it was important to set aside some traditions for a time and let some traditions go away completely. In many ways, death brings clarity to our lives. It is the kind of clarity that helps us to see what is important and what is not.

Instead of packing each moment full of traditions and activities, I found it was far more important to slow down and enjoy the simplicity of the season, just being together. I had to give myself permission to let go of the traditions or activities that were no longer a good fit for our family in each changing season. This was a little hard for me, even as the kids grew up and left home. I had to allow myself to enjoy the memories of each tradition or activity, without hanging onto those things way past their usefulness. At first, creating new traditions and discontinuing old ones felt like letting go of part of Nicole since we had done some of those things all her life. However, over time I realized it was healthy to let go of some of the activities and it caused me to honor Nicole's memory in beautiful new ways. It also freed me up to enjoy new traditions and activities that fit with our current life.

Just like the purple balloons on her birthday, I've found ways to honor Nicole in our new traditions. For instance, there is always a touch of purple intertwined with our Christmas decorations. If I can stick a butterfly in somewhere, that is even better. Purple and butterflies are symbols of Nicole's life here and the impact that she made and is still making.

My friend Terri and her family have one such tradition that honors their daughter Heather's birthday. The year after Heather passed away, a friend of theirs named Doug was sick and it just happened to be Heather's birthday. Terri and her husband Bill gave blood for Doug and a seed was planted. The next year Doug was still sick, so this time they took pizza and more family. Year after year, the tradition has blossomed and grown into something their family could have never imagined. Liz, who is an amazing, bold young woman became the cheerleader because of her own experiences. She had grown men crying, as she explained that she wouldn't be there if it hadn't been for heroes like them. Hence the movement caught the name "Heather's Heroes". That year the blood bank committed to booking a bus for Heather's Heroes. Last year, because of so many donations, the blood bank ended up sending two buses. Now individuals from several states, including Utah, Colorado, Texas, Nevada, Wyoming and Idaho gather around Heather's birthday to honor her memory and pay it forward. Heather's Heroes collect an average of forty-five to fifty units of blood each year. Now, instead of sadness on Heather's birthday, Terri has hope. She told me that God lifts burdens off her heart every year.

Terri's is a great example of turning a potentially hard day into a beautiful day. I wish I could say I have done all this perfectly over time, but I can't. I still get lost in the layers of my grief and have to step back and remind myself of what is important. I know there is always a pull on me to conform to what our culture deems important and have to fight to slow down, breathe and focus on what is truly important.

A sweet friend from church gave me a Christmas ornament every year in memory of Nicole. For ten years as Christmas approached, Cindy would hand me a gift bag that held a beautiful ornament adorned with Nicole's name and the year. Now, I can't help but smile when I get ready to decorate the Christmas tree and see the wide array of ornaments given in kindness. It reminds me that Nicole is not forgotten and I am loved.

I am so thankful for the people God has sent to our family who have carried us through the hard years of transitioning through the birthdays and holidays. They have taught us what true friendship looks like and it encourages me to be that kind of friend.

- *Grief Note:* Slow down, do less and be present.
- *Grief Note.* When you are facing the first of a difficult holiday without your child or loved one, give yourself space to mix it up. Don't allow the expectations of the culture to define what is best for your family. If you are like us and can't stand the thought of being home during that first holiday or occasion, go somewhere new. Or give yourself the freedom not to celebrate or decorate at all. There will be time later to pick up the traditions that you want to or even to create new ones. Just give yourself room to grieve and to allow God to bring healing and comfort to your heart.
- *Grief Note.* Find what works for you and your family. Creating traditions that include serving others is a beautiful way to honor our kids, but also help us to look outside ourselves and our own pain. Make a Christmas box for a needy child or sing Christmas Carols at a Convalescent Hospital. Serve at a local rescue mission or pediatric cancer unit at your local hospital. It is hard

to get lost in our own grief when we are serving others. When you look to someone else's needs, it frees you to look past your own pain. Proverbs 11:25 says, "The man who gives much will have much, and he who helps others will be helped himself."

- *Love Them Well.* If you know someone is grieving a major loss, do not to stay away or avoid them as a holiday or special occasion approaches. It may feel awkward, so it is easy to steer clear of them because you don't want to do or say the wrong thing. Show up, invite or call them on their loved one's birthdays or significant holidays. Allow flexibility for them to come for part of the time or decline if they are not up to it at all. The most important thing is that you make yourself available. Sometimes we feel like we need to speak words that will take away their pain, but there are no words to do that. Some of the biggest comfort I've ever received is when no words were spoken at all. If it is Christmas and your friend is alone, invite them to join you.

- *Love Them Well.* Say their loved one's name. You might not want to mention it, for fear of "reminding" them of their loss. They are always aware of the loss and most of the time, they are much more worried their loved one will be forgotten. I love to hear other people talk about Nicole and share special memories of her. My friend Nellie would send me letters, not just on birthdays or holidays, but throughout the year. She would write about how she was thinking of Nicole and how the thought encouraged her.

Chapter 13:

The Rest of The World Moves On

*"There is a time for everything, and a season for every
activity under the heavens"*
(Ecclesiastes 3:1).

Nicole's friends wore purple ribbons on their wrists to remember her and some of her horse friends had silver pins made to wear that bore her initials. I could spot a purple ribbon or a DNP pin from a mile away and felt an instant connection to the wearer. These symbols of their love for Nicole caused a very special bond throughout our close-knit community of friends. Her good friend Stacy called her Nickel and would place nickels on her headstone at the cemetery. It caught on and every time I went to the cemetery there would be a growing amount of nickels along with the flowers left by her friends.

A young man in Nicole's senior class sketched a beautiful picture of her for the year book to go along with a wonderfully written tribute to her. There were scholarships, classes at horse shows and belt buckles, all in Nicole's name. The outpouring of love for our girl was humbling. We had an extraordinary support system and their heartfelt gestures honored Nicole's memory well. But the intensity of it all was not sustainable.

Time moves on, life changes and people grow older. Everything here on earth is bound and defined by time. We measure our lives by the time that passes every year. Since Nicole was seventeen when she passed away, she would always be seventeen to me. Her friends got older, as expected. Then her younger siblings became older than she was. That was strange to me. It wasn't as evident at first. But as Nicole's senior class was getting ready to graduate, I became painfully aware of it. It was just four months after her death when our school's administration approached us about honoring Nicole at graduation. We thought it was a beautiful way to remember her and were touched they wanted to do it.

As the evening for the graduation ceremony neared, I doubted our decision to attend. It was going to be excruciating watching her peers walk up the aisle to accept their diploma. I couldn't imagine attending, but I couldn't stand the thought of not going. We decided to move forward with the plan and made arrangements to go.

When we arrived at the Performing Arts Center at our local college, I had to force myself to get out of the car. A somber hush came over the room as we made our way to our reserved seats. The school had graciously saved seats for us in the front of the packed auditorium. I almost felt sorry for the other parents who were excited about their graduating seniors, but were trying to be considerate of us.

The graduating class was small, so it was an intimate occasion. Our hearts were heavy, mixed with grief and gratitude as our eyes landed on the chair draped with Nicole's cap and gown. It was a thoughtful gesture to remind all in attendance that one would be missing. The school honored our girl with such grace and compassion. I am so grateful God allowed us to be in such a school, for such a time. We were not just a number to them, they grieved with us and they celebrated the rest of her class's graduation into the next chapter of their lives.

As the ceremony concluded, there were hugs and tears as everyone left the building. I pretended not to think about the celebratory dinners and parties that were about to take place. It was difficult to congratulate Nicole's classmates and families as we parted that night. It was just the first of many graduations, bridal showers, weddings and baby showers that I would be a part of to remind me of the great void in my heart. As hard as it was, I'm grateful to the school for acknowledging Nicole. It was an important part of the grieving process for us.

I know it was an extremely difficult decision for many of our friends on whether or not to invite us to their celebrations after graduation. I imagine they debated because they understood that inviting us to their parties could possibly worsen our grief, yet they didn't want to leave us out. I am so thankful for those brave souls who communicated with me and continued to include me. My presence at such events was also a painful reminder to them of what they had lost, especially in the early years. And sometimes my attendance would cause the focus of the celebration to be shifted in part to Nicole's memory.

For me, I'm glad I chose to be a part of our friend's celebrations, even though they were difficult and painful. When I would leave those events, I could barely make it out of the door without breaking down. It sometimes would take me days to recover to a place where I could function, but I believe it helped me to acknowledge the deep loss from all our lives. Although attending took me precariously close to the pit of despair, I feel when I embraced the grief and the fragility of life, it brought the pain to the surface and helped usher in healing. I have found that when I have had the courage to take God's hand in these situations, He helps navigate me away from the edge.

It is always hard on both sides as life goes on without our loved ones, but I've really been blessed by wonderful people who have taught me what true friendship looks like. One that really stands out to me is when Nicole's dear friend Mandy got married. Mandy and Nicole were two peas in a pod and they were so very good for each other. They confided in one another and shared their love for horses. So, when I was invited to Mandy's wedding a few years after Nicole went to Heaven, my heart was pierced. I was so grateful I was included, but also anxious about witnessing another celebration without Nicole. Her mom was so sweet and gracious to me, never expecting anything from me, while acknowledging the absence of Nicole and how painful it must be. I chose to go alone to the wedding and arrived to find a seat on the center aisle. I remember feeling blessed that they chose to have an outdoor wedding in a beautiful setting. As you've gathered by now, I am an outside girl and that is when I feel the most freedom. The weather was beautiful and I was reflective as I sat on the white folding chair on the aisle, taking in the beautiful surroundings. I remember imagining Nicole being a part of the wedding party as she helped Mandy get ready for her day. I had to balance those thoughts with reminders to myself that Nicole was in Heaven and I would see her again someday.

As the music shifted to signify that the wedding was about to begin, I could picture Nicole walking up the aisle with the other bridesmaids. I began to pray for comfort and for the Lord to remind me that Nicole was fully alive with Him. About that time, a colorful butterfly gently floated down the aisle above the white runner. I smiled as I thanked God for that wonderful gift. Butterflies symbolize a transient beauty and had become a tangible sign for me of Nicole's life. It was as if God was acknowledging Nicole's absence, but reminding me that she was fully free and alive in Heaven.

As happens, time passes and children grow up. Loss causes us to become acutely aware of the fragility of life. I have found embracing each passing graduation, wedding and birth doesn't have to take away from Nicole's memory. Her memory actually enriches each one through her legacy of love and friendship. I could miss Nicole in each of these events while enjoying the sacred new season that is put before me.

As each new season brings changes and Nicole's friends and siblings move on, it is important for me to quietly acknowledge Nicole. It may not be apparent to others that I am even thinking about Nicole. (Just a side note, I think about Nicole every day. All moms who have lost children do. Our children are a part of us and thoughts of them are always just below the surface.) I am always looking for butterflies and the Lord sends them to me in the craziest, most impossible situations. There have been times I have seen them in cold weather, when there is no way they should be able to survive. When I see them, I may not be in a position to outwardly acknowledge them, but I can smile and feel the Lord give me a squeeze.

We have found ways to incorporate Nicole into our significant celebrations that help ease the sadness of missing her. When

Megan married Jonathan, I was ecstatic. But I had the usual pressing on my heart, wishing that Nicole could be there to see her youngest sister get married. Nicole was crazy about her and always her biggest advocate. She would have been very proud of her and would have loved to be a part of the wedding. We were blessed to find a beautiful outdoor venue at the base of a Southern California mountain range. The setting was idyllic with the ceremony by a small lake and the reception under a pavilion on the hill. My sister-in-law Cindy designed all the decorations and flowers, which created an even more enchanted atmosphere. She tucked silk butterflies into several of the arrangements to honor Nicole.

When Megan was pregnant with her and Jonathan's first child, our first grandchild, I was still grieving over the loss of my mom a few months earlier. I was missing my mom and so sad that she would not be able to see her first great-grandchild. As grief sometimes does, it multiplied and caused me to miss Nicole more than usual. I could imagine Nicole as an amazing aunt and spoiling Megan's kids. I had to push the thoughts of "what could have been" out of my mind so I could open myself up fully to the wonderful season of new life in our family.

The weather was beautiful as we prepared for Megan's baby shower under the shade of the expansive weeping willow tree in our backyard. I felt anxious as I fussed over the details as well as struggling with the sorrow of missing my mom and Nicole on such an important occasion. I prayed for the Lord to calm my heart and if he would, for Him to please send me a butterfly as comfort and assurance. I am not even kidding when I say that day was filled with butterflies! Not just one, but several bright yellow Desert Swallowtail butterflies hung out with us that day. I can't begin to describe how magical it was. Several of the guests asked if I had released butterflies for the shower. I laughed as I told them God had done that just for me.

Not every life milestone is filled with butterflies and I don't always embrace the changing seasons the way I should. But, if I am able to give myself room to miss those that have gone on before me, like my parents and Nicole, while still allowing myself to celebrate the beautiful moments of life, I do better.

Time marches on and people grow up and away. As I've watched Nicole's friends move on with their lives, I have had to set them free in my own mind. I know I have had the tendency at times to hold on to them. In some ways it has made me feel close to Nicole. They all have been very gracious to me and I'm still in contact with many of them.

When I'm able to look at the positives and the blessings of change, then I am able to embrace the many blessings that come with change. Our family continued to grow after Nicole went to Heaven. The Lord allowed us to have foster children come to stay in our home. That really opened our eyes to the lost children in our foster care system. Our daughter Jessica was one of those kids, when she came to stay with us for a long-term placement. Although we did not get to legally adopt her, she is still a part of our lives and has given us a beautiful little grand girl Eliana. Lisa, who still deeply misses Nicole, has grown up to be a beautiful young lady and is pursuing her dream to start her own business. Megan married Jonathan and has given us four amazing little grandkids. Alex married his sweetheart Hannah, whom we absolutely love. Nicole and Hannah would have been great buddies and co-conspirators. We were able to adopt two more boys after Nicole went to Heaven. Andrew and Max are biological brothers and have brought so much fun to our lives. Andrew married Bethany, whom we also love. They have given us another incredible grandson and granddaughter on the way. Even though Andrew and Max never got to meet Nicole, they are connected to the fact they have a sister in Heaven. The kids have carried on the butterfly tradition and every wedding has had a butterfly tucked in here and there. Max was born just about two months after Nicole went to Heaven. We feel that he is a special gift to us. Every changing season marks a world that has moved on, but it has also changed my perspective. Blessings abound in change, I just have to be watching for them.

- *Grief Note.* As you receive invitations to events of your loved one's peers, you may find yourself declining to attend. You may feel too raw to even consider it and I understand. Every situation is unique, so prayerfully consider what is healthiest for your heart.

- *Grief Note.* Don't be afraid to look for the blessings. As you start looking, and even asking God, for physical symbols of His love and faithfulness, whatever they are, He will reveal Himself. And often He reveals Himself in the most unusual and unlikely of places.

- *Love Them Well.* If you are agonizing about whether to include a grieving friend in some of life's milestones in your life, I would encourage you to include them always. Yet communicate there are no expectations. When it is time for the event, do just that, have no expectations. Always give them space for the expression of their hearts. They need to feel safe in order to attend. They may need to be quiet and sit in the back or have the freedom to laugh and enjoy without judgement. They may need to leave suddenly, so leave room in your plans for that possibility. I would also suggest if you plan on making their loved one's loss a part of whatever event you are planning, talk to them ahead of time and ask their permission. You may feel whatever you are planning may be honoring to the family, but it may only complicate their pain and attendance. It is important they don't feel blindsided by a gesture that you mean well toward them.

Chapter 14:

Aftershocks

"'Though the mountains be shaken and the hills be
removed, yet my unfailing love for you will not be
shaken nor my covenant of peace be removed,' says the
LORD, who has compassion on you"
(Isaiah 54:10).

When we lose someone we love, grief doesn't wrap itself up in a neat little package and give us all the time we need to heal and become steady in our lives again. The rhythm of life often resembles the earth during and after a catastrophic earthquake. During an earthquake, the surface of the earth can violently shake and move until everything you thought you had put away in a nice, neat little life is strewn into a senseless mess. When the ground stops shaking, and you feel like you are just beginning to steady your legs underneath you, often you are hit with more shaking. Aftershocks. Sometimes the aftershocks after an earthquake are almost as powerful as the original earthquake.

This is how I felt after I lost Nicole. We have already established, grief isn't something you heal from or fix. It is something you learn to walk through. For me, the brutality of grief came when I felt the shaking ground began to settle, and felt somewhat steady, then I was hit with aftershocks of other losses.

The word "grief" is normally associated with the death of someone we love. Although death normally ushers in the most severe form of grief, there are many other losses that cause our hearts to go through the grieving process. The loss of dreams, a betrayal, or the aftershock of more death compounds our pain in grief.

The year after Nicole went to Heaven it felt as if I attended more funerals than I had in my entire life. I'm sure that wasn't the case, but it felt like it. With each service I attended, I felt my life shaking like an aftershock. I reasoned it was because it was so close to the loss of Nicole. However, because we do live in a world that experiences constant loss and regeneration, the losses continued. When I lost my parents (within a few years of each other) I really struggled. I felt like something was wrong with me because I couldn't go back to ground zero after each loss. Again, it was sorrow upon sorrow shaking my world and even though it looked as if I was fine on the outside, my spirit was a mess.

Some of the losses I experienced were harder to recover from than others. Some people didn't understand my pain and dismissed it as extreme. Not everyone will get you or understand you. Some people may even tell you that you should be "over it" or it's "time to get on with your life". I tried to explain to someone the feeling of being "orphaned" after my mom died and was dismissed. How can an adult woman be orphaned? Again, not everyone will be able to relate to how you are feeling during the pain of these aftershocks.

Grief tends to bring out either the best or the worst in people. It is usually not conscious. But many times, true colors are revealed through tragedies. Relationships can change. Some relationships have simply outlived their necessity and quietly drift away. There were several friends of Nicole's with whom we stayed in touch for a bit after she passed. With some, it was too painful, both for them and for us. It was in the best interest of all our healing processes to let go. It wasn't easy, but it also wasn't a devastating fall-out. Yet it still hurt.

Other times, relationships may turn ugly. The people you knew and loved and trusted will change. Sometimes it's over money, other times it's over expectations of how grief should look and be walked out by one another. Raw emotions may lead to unfiltered words or deeds. As you grieve your loved one, you may also grieve these lost relationships or unkind words.

I told a friend of mine who had also lost a child that when we lost our daughters, it was as if we were thrust into another dimension. We could see and function with everyone else, but we would feel things differently, more radically because of our experience. Not better, not worse, just different. I don't know if that is the experience with everyone who has lost a child, but it has been a common thread with the women I've talked to.

Loss of dreams can also cause us to be pressed into an aftershock of grief. The loss of a career we have worked all our lives for, a spouse that walks away after many years of marriage, a struggling adult child that distances themselves from the family, or fractured relationships. All of these can represent a loss of a dream and cause the ground to shake beneath us.

Grieving over all of these is a natural response to loss. It is important that we accept the process and embrace the sorrow we feel, to ensure we are coping in a healthy way. I do believe balance is the key, because to give in completely to our pain can push us into despair and depression. On the contrary to bury our emotions and not deal with our grief can just prolong the process. Sadly, it took me a while to strike that balance and I began to develop some unhealthy patterns.

I began to realize the aftershocks of life caused me to have a sort of grief PTSD. Instead of ever easing, I continually felt on high alert, as if I could eliminate pain or ease the shock when I was faced with the inevitable crisis. I don't think I consciously did it. I think I became so used to anxiety and heartache that I didn't know how to function without it. Every phone call would spike my adrenaline, especially in the middle of the night. When an ambulance passed, I became increasingly anxious, having the urge to call my family members to make sure they were okay. When each kid would reach driving age, the tension and pressure on my heart would sometimes consume me. I am so thankful for my patient kids, because every time they would drive somewhere, I would make them text or call me at every stop and before they started home.

When I had to go out of town, these feelings were ramped up exponentially. I tried to arrange every detail for the house and the animals, making extensive lists for whoever was caring for them. I had created a thought process that every time I left town, something bad happened. When something went wrong or not exactly as I had planned while I was gone, it just confirmed my feelings.

As you can imagine this detrimental way of living began to rob me of my health, my sanity and my joy. The reality was that sometimes bad things did happen and life did throw me curve balls. 1 Peter 4:12 says, "Dear friends, do not be surprised at the fiery ordeal that has come on you to test you, as though something strange were happening to you."

And Matthew 5:45 says, "the rain falls on righteous as well as the unrighteous."

No amount of worrying or anxiety could control the perceived good or bad that came into my life. Because we live in a fallen world, we live amongst the effects of fallenness.

James 1 reminds us struggling can produce perseverance, which leads to maturity. I desperately wanted to be mature. Instead of becoming mature and complete, I became trapped in my anxiety and was living in a constantly tense state. Not only did that harm my health, but it rendered me useless and ineffective. I remember really wanting to make every moment in my life count. I wanted to make Nicole, my mom and my dad proud of me. Most of all, I wanted the Lord to be proud of me, because I knew I would come face to face with Him some day.

I still struggle with anxiety because of the what-ifs. I have learned to listen to the Lord whispering to my heart when I start down that road. The earlier I listen, the easier it is to manage the anxiety. I have to ask myself, "Why am I anxious right now?" Sometimes there is absolutely nothing to be anxious about. Sometimes I may have some hard thing looming. But then I have to remind myself that no amount of anxiety is going to solve the hard situation I may be facing. As a matter of fact, it normally makes it worse because anxiety hinders us from thinking clearly.

So, if this was the way of life on this earth, I had to create a battle plan that would help me to remain balanced and healthy. I wish I could say I am super diligent about practicing the following disciplines daily, but I can't. I will say when I am intentional about this, I am able to live a healthier, balanced life with more clarity and purpose.

Be Grateful. When I am grateful and choose to count my blessings, it begins to push out the anxiety to which I have become accustomed. The longer I've entertained anxiety and worry, the more I have to push through and think about my blessings. I may have to say them out loud, write them down or review them in my mind. But eventually, thankfulness pushes out anxiety and ushers in peace. Gratitude anchors my spirit to the present. 1 Thessalonians 5:18, "Give thanks in all circumstances; for this is the will of God in Christ Jesus for you." There is always something to be grateful for. In Ann Voscamp's book *One Thousand Gifts* she wrote, "Thanksgiving is necessary to live the well, whole, fullest life."

Some days it may be harder than others to identify something to be grateful for. When I am in one of those times, I bring it down to the simplest of terms. The way the sun feels on my shoulders or the shelter of my home are wonderful examples of simple things. However, as Christ followers, even on our darkest days, we have the assurance this is not all there is and He has rescued and saved us. What greater cause for gratitude is there?

Be Present. I've found it helpful to be intentional about scheduling brief moments throughout my day to stop and take in the beauty of now. During those times, I turn off the noise, even music and just listen. I purposely allow my senses to take in what is around me. Because I love to be out in nature, if the weather is cooperating, I will try to go outside. I live in Tennessee, so my favorite time to do this is in the summer months about 7:45 p.m. The fireflies are starting to come out as the sun is going down. I call it the magic hour. I walk down our long driveway and take in God's magical display.

We are not always in a beautiful setting and able to enjoy the magic hour, but we can be present wherever we are. It may be in the smile of a child or a flower at the edge of a sidewalk. Something else may speak to you, but the important thing is to stop and take in where you are. Soak in now.

If I am always looking to the future of the what-ifs, my worry and anxiety will always get the best of me. Sometimes it is hard to be present where we are because we are holding on to what-ifs of the past. It may be someone else's choice to walk away or some unmet dream or expectation. Most of what I am worried about will never happen or will be so completely different that I could never anticipate it in the first place. No amount of worrying and anxiety will undo what has happened in the past or change the future. A simple, yet profound axiom that has spoken to my life is, "Don't borrow trouble." (A paraphrase of Matthew 6:34).

Love and Let Go. I have also learned to love others effectively, I need to let go of expectations of how they will receive my love. Can I love people, leaving the outcome to God? The aftershock effects of other people's decisions can paralyze me in my desire to rescue or fix them. While it is important we are outward focused, loving people, it is equally important we don't try to save them from God working in their lives. It's easy to worry about where their decisions will take them and stress about the harmful consequences they may have to suffer.

You may not do this, but I sure do. In all reality, it is arrogant for me to think it is my responsibility to fix and rescue those I love. I don't have all the answers and I'm not God. The Lord has taken me on my journey and is still constantly teaching and guiding me. Why should I expect it to be any different for others? Let go of the choices that are not yours to be made. Let go of what you can't change or make a difference in. We are not responsible for the outcome of the choices of others.

If you are living and breathing, chances are you've experienced a significant loss or sorrow in your life. Also, chances are it wasn't just one isolated instance and you have had to live through the shaking of your world due to aftershocks. Aftershocks caused because of disappointments, betrayals or continual loss of those you love. Because you are tired of the shaking, you may be experiencing a form of grief PTSD like I did. It may leave you shaken up and worn out, finding it difficult to function. Starting your day with the Lord, practicing gratitude, being present and loving while letting go can steady your quaking heart in the midst of a shaking world.

- *Grief Note.* Understand the loss of dreams and relationships will cause you to grieve. Take the time to mourn those losses as well. But, just like the initial quake of grief, keep journeying through the process. Remember when others speak or act out of pain, it is their pain that is speaking. Do not place their burdens or expectations upon your shoulders. Instead, thank God for the season of blessings when the relationship was sound, and surrender it to Him.

- *Grief Note.* Start the day with Jesus. It may sound churchy or cliché, but it is so true. Before the voices and demands of everyday life start pressing in, it is important that I hear from the Lord. This doesn't have to be an elaborate, lengthy daily program. But I do believe it is important to do it in the morning. It can be as simple as reading a verse and spending some time in prayer. I am currently using an app on my phone that reads a scripture and expounds on the verse. I have also gone through several devotional books that lists a scripture and then has a brief inspirational section about it. One of the most helpful devotions I've completed several times is *Streams in the Desert* by Mrs. Charles Cowman. In the beginning of my grief, my concentration was very limited, so it was important that I kept it simple. Now I find I can be more detailed. It is just important for me to look to Jesus first thing, before I look to any other source.

- *Love Them Well.* As you walk with someone in the aftershocks of their grief, have patience. They are not taking steps back in their journey of grief. They are just experiencing new or unexpected facets of it. Telling someone to get over it or move on is detrimental and painful.

Chapter 15:

Use Your Pain

"Praise be to the God and Father of our Lord Jesus
Christ, the Father of compassion and the God of all
comfort, who comforts us in all our troubles, so that we
can comfort those in any trouble with the comfort we
ourselves receive from God"
(2 Corinthians 1:3–4).

Prior to Nicole going to Heaven, I had signed up for a Bible Study class called Divine Surrender. I had intentions of taking the class months earlier but kept putting it off because of my busy schedule. In hindsight, I see God's hand at work with His perfect timing. It was no coincidence that it started shortly after Nicole went to Heaven. I saw Lori, the leader of the class in the hall of church and she asked me if I was still planning to be there. I was hesitant because I felt like I was not up to participating in the class in my fragile condition. Lori encouraged me to be there and assured me she would put me in a small group where I could feel "safe" in my grief. Then she went on to say something that has stuck with me since. She said, "Kim, it is important that you use your pain." At first, I was taken aback, as was one of my other friends who heard the exchange. It felt like a harsh statement spoken out of an insensitivity to my situation, especially since Nicole had only recently passed away.

I didn't know it at the time, but Lori was no stranger to traumatic grief and understood something I was not ready to grasp yet. (Her own brother had recently passed away tragically.) Using my pain would bring about healing, not only to me, but to others as well.

I did end up attending Divine Surrender and I believe it was one of the major ways God taught me to walk through my pain. Lori was a great, straight forward leader and did indeed create a "safe" small group within that Bible Study for me. I didn't know all the women when we started the group, but through our time meeting together, our hearts were connected in a way that created lasting friendships. Each week those women surrounded me without judgement and loved me. I didn't realize how important it was for me to have a safe place to be vulnerable in some of my darkest days.

God did, though. It was no coincidence I had committed to attending the Bible Study before Nicole went to Heaven. I also am convinced it is no coincidence I ran into Lori in the hall on that Sunday morning. God knew I would need prompting to follow through with my commitment and He knew I would desperately need the content of the study, as well as the support of the ladies in my group.

Divine Surrender was about exactly that. Surrendering everything to God and developing an open-hands mindset toward

Him, holding nothing back. There were very tender, emotional moments that took place during the study as we opened the Bible and learned what true surrender really meant. It was a hard message for this mama who had just lost her first-born daughter. I felt like I had already had to give up so much, would God really expect more of me? I learned how to take my pain and sorrow off the altar and put God on the altar of my heart. Being raised in church I was familiar with all the principals, but having just lost Nicole, I was forced to examine them in the light of my grief.

God did truly show me how to "use my pain" during that session at Bible study and gave me the opportunity fairly soon to practice it. Lori had scheduled a night of testimonies, where she chose three women to share what God was teaching them and how it applied to their lives. She asked me to be one of those women. I was afraid of speaking publicly anyway, but to speak of losing my child in such a personal way seemed terrifying. In the past, I was so opposed to speaking publicly that, in high school, I was willing to take an F because I refused to give an oral current event presentation for the class. I had spoken briefly to the youth of our church during a prayer meeting after Nicole died, but that was the extent of my public speaking experience.

I asked my group to pray for me as I agreed to share my testimony about surrendering the loss of Nicole to the Lord. It was one of the most powerful moments of my life as God spoke through me and helped me to "use my pain". I don't really remember what I said, but I do remember feeling His strength speaking through me. I understood what Lori meant and realized Nicole's death gave me a platform to share God's amazing love and provision. That is where the passion for women's ministry, especially for grieving moms was born. I eventually became a

Bible Study leader for Divine Surrender and was so humbled as the Lord continued to use my story in that forum.

I continued to speak to groups of women over the years, but nothing was as powerful as that first time. It was so amazing for me to experience God's working in me despite my complete inadequate state. The Lord had infused me with His comfort and was continually walking me through the difficult journey of grief. The bereavement I was experiencing had the tendency to become stagnant like a still, standing pool of water. Every time I shared my experience, it was as if a part of the pool was opened to a fresh, free-flowing stream of water. The stream was cleansing and fresh, bringing new life to me and to those exposed to the current.

Please don't get me wrong, it was not me that did the work. I am truly the weakest and wimpiest person around. I have trouble coming up with words to complete a sentence and I am not brave. However, God just needed my willingness to put myself in the place of saying yes. That was terrifying in and of itself. What if I was reading His intentions incorrectly and made a fool of myself? Actually, that did happen a few times, but only when I tried to speak on His behalf on my own power.

Joshua 1:9 kept coming back to me. "Be strong and courageous." It was only possible because He was with me. He would never leave me. As long as I relied on Him and not on myself, God grew me in the area of women's ministry. I was blown away with how He allowed me to use my pain. "He comforts us in all our troubles, so that we can comfort others. When they are troubled, we will be able to give them the same comfort God has given us" (2 Corinthians 1:4).

The comfort God brought to me flowed over and brought the same comfort to others. For me, because of my experience, I felt drawn to hurting women, especially those who had lost a child.

Many amazing movements have been started because brave individuals were willing to use their pain to help ease the pain of others. Not everyone who has lost a child should lead a Bible Study group or become grief counselors. Not every cancer survivor should serve those struggling with cancer. Those who are widowed don't necessarily have to set up ministries. The 2 Corinthians verse says we are to flow out comfort from the comfort that we've been given, but that can manifest itself in many ways. God plants various seeds in our hearts through our pain that grow to be a beautiful garden when cultivated in our own unique ways.

Maybe because your child is a cancer survivor, you are drawn to ministering to children and are called to be a teacher. It might be that people brought meals for your family during a crisis and it sparked a passion for you to lead the Helps Ministry in your church. The verse says, "with the comfort that you've been given," and we are all comforted in unique and special ways.

For me, the Lord knew I needed to be immersed in the Divine Surrender Bible Study and Women's Ministry fairly quickly after Nicole's accident. I don't know why, but maybe I would have given in to my pain and become stagnant. Being involved in the way I was helped me tremendously. However, I know this isn't the case for everyone. Some individuals need an extended time away from service for their healing and that is okay. God knows each of us individually and intimately and will present opportunities as He sees fit. The time table the Lord uses in every person's heart will be uniquely created for their growth and His glory.

We also must be very careful about the expectations we have about our particular passions. It is the Lord who plants the seeds in our hearts and it is Him that causes those seeds to grow in the most productive way. Consequently, it is the Lord that uses us to plant the seeds of comfort in the hearts of others and His responsibility to grow it in them as He sees fit.

I had to learn the hard way not to try to take responsibility for the growth of that seed in others. I sometimes became frustrated when they didn't respond in the way I felt they should or appreciate my help. My only responsibility is to seek God and be sensitive to the direction in which He is calling me to minister. Sometimes it is in a tender, sensitive place that may bring up pain. When that happens, He is faithful to take care of me. The world is full of broken people and unless I'm willing to be broken in that world, there won't be healing. It is not me that is doing the work, it is God through me. It is the act of laying my broken heart on the altar before God and being willing to say yes.

Another example of following where God calls us to go may literally mean going. In 2014, our family packed up and moved across the country to Tennessee. It was hard to move away from all we had known. It was hard to leave the place Nicole's earthly body now laid, along with the remains of my parents, who are buried near her. But God never calls us without a plan. The blessings of the move to the Nashville area have been so much more than I could have asked or imagined. There is a different kind of beauty, a different kind of nature to wrap myself in, and a different kind of healing that continues to my soul. (Not to mention...there are grandkids here!)

My friend Terri lost her sweet daughter Heather in a terrible traffic accident. She had many people come to offer support and comfort during those hard days. Terri told me that for her, it was very important to say thank you to every person that helped her family. As you can imagine, that was an impossible task, because of the enormity of the amount of people that were there for her. In the fogginess of grief, it is hard to remember everything and even to grasp all that people are doing for you. It is sometimes after the fact that you become aware of the presence of so many of the people that were near to offer comfort. Being able to thank everyone individually was important to Terri and it made her feel helpless when she couldn't. Terri said one way she could show gratitude for all that was done for her during her hardest days was to "pay it forward" by helping others. Her attitude of paying it forward is what led her to become a 9-1-1 dispatcher. Some people could never imagine being a 9-1-1 dispatcher after what Terri had endured. You can imagine during those especially distressing calls, she may be reminded of Heather's accident. But that is not the way Terri sees it. She says, "I get to fulfill that (paying it forward) every single day, one 9-1-1 call at time. It's not people that say thank you or are even grateful…at least outwardly. Sometimes it is almost good for me to have people like that. I have to dig deep to help them anyway. It's almost penance in some way."

Terri knows how important the communication between frightened, traumatized people and the first responders are. She has had to handle some very difficult situations, but she has also had some blessings, like the time she helped guide the delivery of the baby of one of her former 4-H members in the Target parking lot. She believes that every call is a Divine appointment and there are no coincidences. In this way, she is "using her pain."

As a timid high school student, I would have never imagined I would be doing what I am today. I could not have fathomed I would be using the pain of losing a child to help other people. It is definitely not me or on my own strength. God has given me the courage to do what I thought I could never do. Joshua 1:9 tells us to be strong and courageous, not because we can conjure up strength and bravery on our own, but because "the Lord will go with me wherever I go."

One of the pastors at our church, Chris Nicols asked a compelling question a few months ago. He asked, "What would be different if I was convinced God was with me? Would I have the strength to go another round?" I love that. Am I living as if I am convinced God is with me? I would say it this way for the purpose of our subject: What would be different if I was convinced God was with me? Would I have the courage to use my pain to bring comfort to others?

- *Grief Note.* God has used Nicole's passing powerfully and repeatedly in many people's lives. It has not been an easy thing for me to process, allow, or participate with Him. But He has fulfilled His promise that ALL things work together for the good of those who love Him. Allow Him to use your pain. He absolutely does NOT cause pain; but He does love to redeem it for His glory.

- *Love Them Well.* Become the champion, partner, advocate, supporter and cheerleader of someone who is allowing God to use their pain. Walk beside them. Attend events. Hold their hands. Hug them on the hard times.

Conclusion

"God can do anything, you know
—far more than you could ever imagine
or guess or request in your wildest dreams!
He does it not by pushing us around but by working
within us, his Spirit deeply and gently within us"
(Ephesians 3:20, The Message).

When Nicole went to Heaven, I thought the world was literally going to end. I felt as if there was only pain and sorrow everywhere. If someone had told me I would have another thirty to forty years ahead of me on this earth, I probably would have told them to get out of my face. I believed survival was not possible. Over time it became obvious I would be here a while, so God must have a plan for my survival. I decided I better find a way to heal myself in my grief. I decided I would push through my pain, so I could survive.

Now, all these years later, I see even though there has been a large measure of healing in my heart, I will never get over the sorrow of losing Nicole. My heart will never be "fixed" and return to the way I was prior to December 28, 1998. Grief is a part of my life and it has forever changed me, and that's okay. I've learned just surviving is not the plan, but the plan God has for me is for a future and a hope. Not to harm me, but to cause me to flourish and thrive, not despite of my sorrow, but in the midst of it. Over the last nineteen years, He has taken all the broken pieces of my heart and is making them into something beautiful.

There is a uniquely beautiful form of Japanese art called Kintsugi in which the artist mends broken pottery by using a special lacquer mixed with gold, silver or platinum. So, instead of trying to hide the cracks in the piece, the imperfections are accentuated, whereby the flaws become part of the history of the piece. It becomes more beautiful than it was before it was broken. In our culture, broken items are often discarded and considered trash, but the art of Kintsugi focuses on the restoration and value in the broken pieces.

Our earthly lives are like this to the Lord. We sometimes wish He would make our flaws and cracks disappear...until we begin to see the wonderful piece of art He is creating in us, using our broken pieces. Every crack has significance and every flaw is used to showcase the gold that He is bringing forth in our lives.

God has used my pain of losing Nicole and is piecing together a masterpiece I could have never imagined. Not because I'm special or strong, but because He is. You also have a story. No matter where you are in the depths of your sorrow, He is there. He really is. Nicole's death should have destroyed me, but by giving my broken heart to God, He lifted me up. Instead of discarding me because I was broken, He is filling the broken places with beautiful gold.

There are still hard days. I long to see Nicole and hear her voice. I think about Nicole every day. Even when it doesn't show on the outside, she is on my mind. I miss her and still have some of her belongings in crates because I haven't had the heart to open them in a while. I am still a work in progress, and you are, too. I don't know what depths of grief your heart has experienced, whether it is the loss of a child in death, the loss of someone you never imagined living without, or if it is the loss of a dream. But I will tell you that you will make it through this.

The scars, on your heart or on your body, are reminders. They are reminders to others and to ourselves. We are more than survivors. We are conquerors in our battles. We are Victorious.

About the Author

Kim Peacock was thrust into a world she never imagined when her daughter, Nicole, died in a tragic accident. Grappling through the grief has produced and continues to produce a passion to help others navigate the complexities of grief with hope. She is a wife, mother, writer, speaker and grief mentor. Her blog, *Wild Victorious Heart*, has been an encouragement to others during the life-altering loss of a loved one.

She currently resides in Middle Tennessee with her husband, Larry, enjoying God's creation and her children and grandchildren.

Visit her site, follow her stories, or contact her for speaking engagements at <u>www.wildvictoriousheart.com</u> .

References

Barnes, M. Craig. *When God Interrupts: Finding New Life through Unwanted Change.* Downers Grove, IL: Intervarsity Press, 1996.

Cowman, Mrs. Charles E. *Streams in the Desert, 366 Daily Devotional Readings.* Edited by James Reimann. Grand Rapids, MI: Zondervan, 2013.

Mercola, Joseph, DO. "How Exercise Can Help the Grieving Process." Mercola.com. June 27, 2014. Accessed May 18, 2018. https://mercola.com/sites/fitness/archive/2014/06/27/exercise-grief.aspx.

Shedd, John A. *Salt From my Attic.* Portland, ME: Mosher Press, 1928.

Voskamp, Ann Morton. *One Thousand Gifts.* Eugene, OR: Zondervan, 2010.